Table of Contents

This   Book is divided into four sections - each part consist of 101 tips:

<u>Part 1</u> **- 101 Money Saving Tips**

<u>Part 2</u> **- 101 Success Tips**

<u>Part 3</u> **- 101 Health & Fitness Tips**

<u>Part 4</u> **- 101 Romance Tips**

PART 1 - 101 MONEY SAVING TIPS

People are always trying to save money, especially with today's economy. No matter what your reason for saving, through this e-book, you will discover ways never considered.

The price of everything has gone up, requiring people to be more conscientious about money. The problem is that by the time the mortgage, car, utilities, and credit cards are paid, there is little money to put aside. Saving money is not that hard, just a matter of learning all the different options and being creative.

In addition to the obvious of putting money into a retirement fund or savings account, there are hundreds of ways to save money. Although some ways of saving may not seem like much, once you add them up at the end of the year, you will see how substantial the savings really are. Keep in mind that saving is more than a single lump sum of money put aside. Saving is something found in your everyday life by the way you live and the choices you make.

Rome was not built in a day and neither will your bank account be. Each penny saved is one more penny than before. If you have the ability to save big, that is great. However, most people are not in that position, which is why this e-book will show you how little savings can add up quickly.

Be encouraged that it is never too late to start saving, regardless of your age. Set your mind that now is the time to start building your future.

1. *Holiday Gift Giving*

This tip is especially helpful for large families. Although it is fun buying for and receiving from everyone, it can be very expensive. Make an agreement with your family that you will continue to buy for the children but that the adults will go with a name exchange. This way the children are not disappointed and you can spend a little more on one or two people rather than spreading your money thin. For the members that you did not pick to exchange with, bake a loaf of their favorite homemade bread or cookies.

2. *Clearance*

Always head straight for the clearance rack where you can find amazing bargains. Sometimes you may have to dig a little to find the right item but the savings will be well-worth your time. Most clearance racks offer variety, current trends, and great value. For example, Bed, Bath & Beyond has a clearance section where you can find all kinds of wonderful household items for a fraction of the original cost.

3. *Thrift / Surplus Stores*

Unfortunately, thrift and surplus stores have been given a bad rap. Many of these stores are filled with hundreds of top quality items. Name brand merchandise is easy to find but just like clearance racks, it takes some time to find. Find a thrift or surplus store close to where you live and then plan spending some time to find those outstanding bargains. One woman in Kansas City, Missouri located such a store about 20 minutes from her home. After shopping through every isle over the period of two hours, she walked out of the store with eight huge garbage bags filled to the brim with designer clothes for her and her children, many with the original tags still attached. She even found a couple of Liz Claiborne suits for herself at $5.99 each and a Dooney & Burke purse normally valued at $225 for $19.95. Her children had an entire season of school clothes and best of all, she paid less than $200.

4. *Wrapping Paper and Bows*

Create your own wrapping paper, which is not only unique, but also fun. Use plain brown grocery bags and craft-like paints to make your design. After wrapping the gift, let your creative juices flow. For example, using black and yellow craft paint, create a miniature road. Then dipping toy truck tires into red paint roll them along the paper making tire tracks. You can then draw free hand a stop sign, yield sign, or stop light. Next, using a hot glue gun, glue a couple of the miniature trucks to the paper. This is perfect for a young boy. He will be just as thrilled with the wrapping as the actual gift. For a girl, you can simply create miniature bows from existing fabric or lace and glue them on brown paper then free hand draw colorful flowers. Just use your creativity and look around for items you already have on hand to use.

5.   _Reuse_

When you shop, look for items that can be reused. Rechargeable batteries are a perfect example. Even though the initial purchase may be more than non-rechargeable batteries, there is a definite savings over a long period. Another option would be to purchase a nice artificial Christmas tree. Many of the current artificial trees look amazingly real and with the right lights and ornaments, you can change the look from year to year.

6.   _Landscaping_

If you are considering creating a nice flower garden area, shopping for plants even on sale, can be expensive. Before you go out and start spending, look around to see if you have other plants that can be split from your existing flowers. Additionally, if you have a good relationship with any of your neighbors, you might ask them if they have any plants you could use as a starter. Another great idea is the next time you are in the market to buy a lawnmower, purchase one that mulches leaves. This way, rather than buy mulch for your flowerbeds every year, you can simply use the mulch you make.

7.   _Budget_

Everyone should create a budget. If you are not sure how or just not good with money, many businesses such as H&R Block, offer free financial consulting to help you put a budget together. Knowing where you are spending your money is by far the best way to save. In most cases, people have no idea where their money is really going and once they see it on paper, not only are they surprised but eager to change their spending habits.

8. _**Plan**_

Planning is a great way to save. Before you go to the grocery store, make a list and stick with it. If considering a vacation, plan everything. Heading out with no set direction will certainly lead you to impulsive spending.

9. _**Buy in Bulk**_

It is true that warehouse shopping can save a lot of money. Even if you have a small family, you can always split large quantities. The price of items in bulk is generally a great bargain. If you are single, you might go in with friends or family on bulk items.

10. _**Allowance**_

Do not forget to give yourself an allowance for things you enjoy. Even if on a tight budget, buy something that you enjoy, which could be as simple as buying a new shirt or grabbing lunch at your favorite café. If you do not allow yourself this small "splurge", you could find yourself in the same position as if dieting. Total deprivation leads to overindulgence.

11. _**What Matters to You**_

Make a list of the 10 most important things in your life. Next to each item, rank them in order of importance using numbers 1 through 10. The purpose of this exercise is to help you see the things you consider the most and least important and to provide you with a visual of why you need to save. Some examples of things that a person might put on their list include new home, car, special trip, artwork, starting a business, or pay off debts.

12. _**Setting Goals**_

Break your goals into short-term, intermediate-term, and long-term. Being able to see your accomplishments is a great motivator for you to work hard at saving. If you set a short-term goal of saving for tickets to the symphony and reach that goal, you will be encouraged to keep saving for the intermediate and long-term goals.

13. _Be Realistic_

When it comes to saving money, make sure the goals you set for yourself are realistic. If you earn $50,000 a year, saving $20,000 would be nice but it is very unrealistic. Make your goals attainable or you will never save.

14. _Flexibility_

Once you have set your goal for saving, realize that things can and will change. The secret is learning ways to be flexible. If you normally save $150 a month, when something unexpected happens, you may only be able to save $50 that month. This is fine as long as you focus on getting back on track.

15. _Insurance_

Shop around for insurance and work with a good agent that can provide information on discounts such as good student, multi-car discount, etc. Some people think the price of insurance is the same from one company to the next. However, prices can vary dramatically and to ensure you get the best deal, you need to consider all your options.

16. _Coupons_

Okay, maybe you used to laugh as you watched people pull out their coupons at stores but the truth is that using coupons can save you hundreds of dollars every year. Coupons can be used at grocery stores, retail chains, any store where the item is sold. Some stores offer double coupon days, which is an extra bonus. On average, you could easily save from 5% to 15% on a bill for $100 simply by presenting a coupon. Coupons are not just for food items and by scouring your local newspaper you can find coupons for all sorts of merchandise.

17. *Credit Cards*

Use credit cards only for emergency. Although convenient, credit cards are dangerous and damaging. In addition, if you have a credit card that has a $1,000 balance and you pay only the minimum payment each month, it will take you between 20 and 30 years to pay off that $1,000 balance since the majority of money is going strictly toward the interest and not the principal amount.

18. *Mortgage Payment*

Paying one additional mortgage payment each year, whether in a lump sum or monthly increments, can lower a 30-year loan down to 18 years. If you pay more than one extra payment, the number of years will decrease even more. Since this additional payment will be applied only to the principal and not the interest, you end up saving thousands and thousands of dollars once the home is paid off.

19. *Credit Card Interest*

If you have credit cards and your credit is in good standing, call your credit card company, and ask for your interest rate to be lowered. It is truly that simple. Unfortunately, most people do not even realize this is an option so they never make the call. Just tell the representative that you want a better rate on your credit card and they will take care of your request.

20. *Patience*

Be patient when it comes to saving. This means that you need to accept that it will take time to save and good planning. Be patient and remember that just because you want something, do not rush to buy just to satisfy your urge. Instead, wait for sales in order to get the best price, which in turn will save you money.

21. *Financial Consulting*

Many financial companies and even churches offer outstanding classes on how to manage money. While some of these programs are free, others may have a nominal fee of around $35 to attend but the money is well spent. Another great option is consumer-counseling services. This is a great option for people in over their head with debt. The counselors will work directly with your creditors to lower your balances, interest rate, and establish workable payments that you can afford.

22. *Break old Habits*

Take time to learn the various things that "trigger" your spending. When you are depressed, lonely, sad, anxious, excited, whatever it may be, do you spend more? Once you can identify these triggers then you can learn how to control them. As an example, if you were just laid off from your job, although money is tight, you may have an overwhelming "need" to spend money. Perhaps you notice that when you are bored, you head for the shops. Knowing what affects you will help you to discipline yourself to find other ways of comfort.

23. *Avoid Temptations*

If you have a particular weakness, stay away from it. If you love to gamble, stay out of the casinos. If you have a weakness for shoes, drive past your favorite shoe store. While avoiding temptation is hard, it is also necessary in order to save money. When you want to give into your temptation, this is the time to use your "allowance".

24. *The Right Time to Shop*

Studies have proven that when shopping while hungry, depressed, tired, and stressed, you buy more. Before you head to the grocery store, eat something. If you are upset or feeling a little blue, calm yourself down or wait until you feel better before you head out to shop. As funny as it may sound, having a clear mind is important when it comes to shopping and spending money.

25. *Make your Own Gifts*

If you ask people if they prefer a store bought or handmade gift, the majority would choose the latter. Handmade gifts are individualized and come from the heart. When you have a birthday, anniversary, baby shower, wedding, or Christmas gift to give, make the gift. For Christmas, you could make a beautiful ornament or door wreath, for a baby shower you could purchase an inexpensive bib pattern and make special bibs, or for a wedding, you could create a wonderful album of photos showing the couples dating life. Other great options include making homemade hot chocolate, soaps, candles, or lotions and placing them in inexpensive glass containers or baskets purchased at a thrift shop. If you use a mason jar, add foam and fabric under the lid for added color, use a label to write the contents and a message of endearment, and wrap a nice piece of ribbon arounc the ridge. The options are endless, so get creative.

26. *Barter System*

Gather friends, family, neighbors, and co-workers and set up a bartering system. Offer babysitting to one family in exchange for them mowing your lawn or offer to clean someone's house in exchange for a week of car-pooling your child to school. You would be amazed at the opportunities and the money that can be saved using a bartering system.

27. *Matinee*

Do you love the movies but hate the prices? Switch your nighttime show to the late afternoon or early evening matinee. The price is about 50% less and when taking an entire family, that is a nice savings. Pop your own popcorn, put in a plastic bag, and place in a large purse and make or buy your own candy, leaving only drinks to buy. Food at the theater is outrageously priced. The next time that you head to the movies, hit the matinee, stuff those jellybeans and licorice sticks in your purse, and enjoy the savings. Also, check for movie tickets online, which can be discounted

28. *Comparison Shop*

Comparison-shopping can make a big difference in the price you pay. You might be looking at a barbecue grill at one place for $350.00 and by making two more stops, find the exact grill or one comparable for $300. In addition, consider the price of items assembled versus unassembled. For example, you might find the barbecue grill unassembled for $250. A couple of hours of "fun" assembling the grill is certainly worth a $100 saving.

29. *Stop Competing with the Jones'*

You do not have to compete with anyone. Be proud of what you have and who you are. If you can only afford an inexpensive sofa from a thrift store, find a nice throw, make a few pillows, and be proud and thankful. Competitiveness is a part of nature and to a degree, healthy. However, when competition creates a buying war to see who can have the "best" when they have no business buying at all, then it becomes damaging. Stick to what you can afford regardless of what anyone else has or pressure you might be feeling.

30. *Sales Clerk Compliments*

Sales clerks are often paid on commission. Therefore, when you walk into a store and try on an expensive suit, you can be guaranteed you will hear several times over how wonderful you look, how great that suit fits you, etc. Because this is how the clerks make their money, they will say whatever it takes to make the sale. You probably do look good but do not allow yourself to be pressured into buying something beyond your means. Know what you want, the price range you can work with, and stick with your own rules, not theirs.

31. *Incentives – Reward Plan*

To help you and your family spend more wisely, set up a system where rewards are given when the rules set forth are followed. For example, if a family decision was made to start making lunch and brown bagging it to work and school instead of paying each day, the incentive might be that if this is followed strictly for one month, the entire family can spend a Saturday at the Zoo or favorite theme park.

32. *Dollar Stores*

Many years ago, dollar stores offered only off brand products or poorly made merchandise. However, that has completely changed. Now you can walk into a dollar store and find the same name brand laundry soap, cleaning supplies, clothing, school supplies, everything for a fraction of the cost. Where a store name brand bottle of laundry detergent might cost $6.50 at a grocery store, you can find the identical product and size at the dollar store for $2.50. Check out your local dollar store and enjoy the mountains of savings.

33. *Don't Give up the Good Stuff*

A misconception is that while trying to save money you have to deal with sub-par merchandise, which is untrue. If you love fresh breads and pastries, visit a bakery thrift store. For your fresh fruits and vegetables, visit your local farmer's market. Try eBay or other auction sites to buy top quality merchandise for a huge discount. Watch for neighborhood garage sales or estate sales and auctions to find items you need. Just because you are looking for bargains as a way of saving money does not mean you have to skimp on quality.

34. *Utilities*

Set up some rules in your home such as turning lights off when leaving the room, having only a parent adjust the air or heat, leaving the doors or windows open when letting either cold or hot air into the house. Utilities are expensive and a great money saver is to monitor how they are used in your home. Another great idea is the investment of buying an energy-efficient hot water heater. If you cannot afford one, lower the setting so you are not heating water so hot. The hotter the setting, the more energy used.

35. _Check the Garbage_

One woman had her teenage daughter clean her room. The daughter proudly did just that, filling two huge trash bags of things she no longer wanted. Out of curiosity, the mother peeked into one of the bags to see what was being thrown away. In shock, she found a new tube of suntan lotion, two perfectly good sweaters, makeup, lotion, a picture frame, hair curlers, all good things. The daughter did not realize that just because the items were of no interest to her, they might be to someone else. After talking to her daughter, the mom turned around and listed the items on eBay, making a $35 profit on her daughter's "junk."

36. _Written Plan_

When a person goes into business, they create a Business Plan, which becomes the blueprint of their business. The same should apply if you are trying to save money. Create a master plan that the entire family can get involved with and learn their role. When you start to spend too much, go back and look at your plan to see where you are messing up and how you can fix it.

37. _Attitude_

Good money management is an acquired skill. As you go forward with the process of saving money, you need to have a good, positive attitude, which is often what will keep you and your family heading in the right direction. If you think you cannot save, then you probably will not. Be determined and stay positive about saving.

38. _Unsecured Creditors_

Make a list of all your unsecured debts along with creditor contact information and payoff amount so you can have an accurate record of how much you owe. Choose one creditor, possibly a credit card, and focus on paying off that bill. Once you have achieved that goal, choose another. Start with the debt that has the highest interest rate since it is the one costing you the most money.

39. *Off-Season*

The next time you plan a vacation, consider off-season. Generally, the prices for airfare, hotel, and cars are substantially lower than traveling during peak time. If you look at all your options, you will find that in many cases, you can come close to the date you would like to travel. As an example, flying to Hawaii through June 8 is considered off-season while June 9 is peak. One day makes a huge difference in price.

40. *Buy versus Rent or Lease*

When looking at homes or automobiles check the rent and lease options. Depending on your particular situation, renting or leasing may be a better financial decision. Weigh all your options and see which choice makes the best sense from a financial standpoint.

41. *Buffet Meals*

When taking the family out to dinner, consider restaurants that have buffets. In many cases, the prices are outstanding and a parent can share with a small child. In addition, many buffets are "all you can eat" and of course, there is something for everyone.

42. *Cable Networking*

If you have a computer upstairs and another downstairs and you use high-speed data, have one of the computers be the primary computer and the other be the backup. This way, you are only charged once for Internet access and a small fee of $10 to $15 a month for the second computer. This is a great bargain!

43. *Proper Maintenance*

Purchase an annual home warranty policy. These policies can run from $350 to $500 a year and offer extremely valuable options. The way most of these policies work is that if you have something break, such as your garage door, dishwasher, air conditioner, etc., for a minimal fee, usually $50 to $100, a serviceperson will come to your home to fix the item. Best of all, if you have five things broken and the same serviceperson is qualified to fix all of them, you are still charged the $50 to $100 fee once, not five times. For your automobile, you might look into purchasing an extended warranty. If you ever need either one of these policies, they will save you tremendous value.

44. *Company Stock / 401K*

Contributing to employee stock options or a 401K plan is a wonderful opportunity to save. Most companies will match your contribution, sometimes dollar for dollar, up to a maximum, generally 6%. From each paycheck, you can have a small amount of money deducted (1%) and up. Over time, that money grows and since the business is providing a match, you get free money.

45. *Family Haircuts*

Look for hair styling shops that offer family deals or learn how to cut hair yourself. Many families take care of their own haircuts and put the money they would have spent aside as a vacation fund. This system works out perfectly.

46. *Wants versus Needs*

Make sure the thing you want to spend your money on is a "need" and not a "want." Sometimes this can seem like a fine gray line but if you stick to the need list, you will spend less.

47. *Refinance*

With interest rates being so low, consider refinancing your home and/or securing a debt consolidation loan. You might have to come up with a new closing cost but once paid, you will have lower payments, better terms, and save thousands of dollars over the years.

48. _Go Generic_

When buying food, try some of the generic items. Unless you or your guests are connoisseurs of fine dining, they will not know if the green beans were generic or a top name brand. Once you add some butter, salt, and pepper, no one will know the difference except you - $79 per can versus $33 per can! People do not realize that many generic brands are actually manufactured by name brand companies, just branded with a different name. In fact, companies such as those that make snack foods will have conveyor belts that run side-by-side – one for the name brand and one for the generic brand. This is quite common and the only difference is the label and price.

49. _Stock Up_

As you shop, if you notice that a brand you and your family use on a consistent basis is on sale for a great bargain, stock up. As an example, if you use a particular type of shampoo costing $4.50 per bottle and you find it on sale for $2.50, go ahead and buy two bottles. You should only do this on items you know will be used.

50. _Shopping for Clothes_

There are many secrets relating to saving money on clothing. As a perfect example, rather than buy a matched suit for $450, buy the pieces separate. This will save you about $100 to $150. Additionally, buy several pieces that can be mixed and matched, giving you six outfits out of four pieces.

51. _Carpool_

In some larger cities, carpooling is required in order to reduce smog. However, regardless of where you live, carpooling can also be a big money saver. Check with co-workers and determine who lives close enough to share a ride. By the end of the year, you will have saved several hundreds of dollars.

52. *Trendy Fashion*

Most people love to dress in the most up-to-date fashion but for those fashions, you pay big bucks. Consider dressing with basics and then emphasis them with trendy accessories. This will save you money on the clothing that is less expensive while allowing you to dress it up.

53. *Free Entertainment*

If you are tired of being bored, you will be pleased to learn that there are hundreds of things to do that do not cost a dime. For example, if you want a little Friday or Saturday night excitement, sign up at your local police department for a "ride-a-long" where you can go on duty with an officer as they respond to real calls. Community colleges are always offering free exercise classes, or coffee shops have poetry readings. Entertainment and having fun does not have to cost anything. Some cities have special areas that are popular on the weekends where you can find free concerts. Check your local paper and college to get a list for your area.

54. *Telephone / Mobile Phone*

First, shop around for the best deals. Second, stay away from all the fun bells and whistles and just stick with the basic plan. Some people have turned to shutting down their home telephone and are now using their mobile phones in place. Since most wireless carriers offer free long-distance, call waiting, call forwarding, caller ID, voicemail, and more, it can do the same as a regular phone but for less. Why have two phones when you can have just one?

55. *Home Remedies*

Before rushing off to see the doctor for a sore throat, try some home remedies or over the counter drugs instead. For a sore throat, butter mixed with ginger and sugar makes a soothing healing pate. A hot toddy before bed is great for a cold. Simply ask your family for their home remedies and try it. Sometimes a simple over the counter medication or herb will do the trick without costing you an expensive doctor's office visit.

56. *Pay on Time*

For every payment you pay late, you are charged a late fee, which can range from $25 to $50 or more depending on the company. Therefore, if you just made a $50 payment but it was paid ate, nothing was paid toward the debt. Instead, the entire $50 went toward an unnecessary fee. To avoid spending unnecessary money, be sure you mail your check in time to avoid these fees.

57. *Insulation*

Hundreds of dollars are wasted every year from the average home due to improper insulation. Make sure there are no drafts coming from your window, door, or fireplace. Ensure your home has the appropriate level of insulation, which will make a HUGE difference in your utility bill.

58. *Cancel Subscriptions*

It is always fun getting your favorite magazine or book in the mail but you should cancel them or at least most of them. If you have several subscriptions, choose one or two to keep and cancel the rest.

59. *Consolidate your Errands*

To save gas, organize your day of errands so you get as much done in an organized manner as possible. Stay in the same geographical area and hit as many of your errands in that area as possible to avoid excessive driving.

60. *Sell your Stuff*

Go through your house and pull together all the items you no longer use. These can include small or large appliances, gardening tools, clothing, makeup, and sporting equipment, whatever you have, and then list them on eBay.com or Halfoff.com. Take the money earned from these sales and put it in your savings account not to be touched.

61. *Turn your Hobby into Money*

Everyone has a skill – find yours and turn it into money. For example, if you have a skill for woodworking, start creating children's toys, or curio cabinets to sell. Perhaps you are computer savvy and could teach a class at your local community college. Find something you enjoy and sell it.

62. *Recycle*

Try a different type of recycling that will save you money. Have you ever received a nice gift that you like from someone but will never use? Rather than take it back to the store for an exchange, consider keeping it to give as a gift to someone else. Another way to recycle is to look around your home. There are always things right in your home that can be used to make nice gift baskets – things you never use. For example, the next time you purchase shower gel where you buy one and get one free, keep one for yourself and set the other one aside for future gift giving. You will find hundreds of ideas so be creative and consider things you purchased but have never used.

63. *Heating and Cooling*

Make sure vents in rooms not being used or the garage are closed. Many people tend to try to heat and cool the entire home. Instead, take the time to close off areas that you are not using. You will save substantial money on your utilities.

64. *Shop Online*

Many online businesses offer great bargains and in some cases, free shipping. Since the Internet is such a competitive market, you can usually find fantastic deals. In addition, many of your favorite businesses where you shop in person have websites that offer even greater savings. Bookstores such as Amazon.com will sell books up to 70% off the original price. Overstock.com is another online business that sells closeout items for fantastic bargains.

65. *Consignment Shops*

Rather than throw out or sell slightly worn clothing or other household items in a garage sale, consider selling them through a consignment shop. You will get a better price for your items and consignment shops are always looking for quality merchandise. Check out Half.com, which is an online consignment shop offering books, movies, computer software, and much more in either new or used condition.

66. *Selling your Home*

If considering putting your home on the market, make sure you work with a reputable realtor. A good realtor versus one that is not as experienced can be the difference of thousands of dollars. A good realtor will know exactly what you need to do to your home to get it in the best selling condition, which in turn will get you more money. In addition, experienced realtors know all the best methods for advertising and selling your home while saving you the most money.

67. *Stay out of the Malls*

If possible, stay away from shopping malls. High-dollar shopping malls have expensive overhead and are designed to sell, sell, sell. Prices are generally higher and in most cases, people walk out with more than they anticipated buying. It is better to shop at stand-alone shops or on the Internet.

68. *Car Shopping*

Shop around for the best price. While you may have your eye on that "perfect" car and want it now, by waiting and looking around, you could be saving yourself a lot of money. In addition, check out other states. If you live within a few hours drive from other cities, check out the price difference. The five hours it takes to drive may be worth the money saved.

69. *Check Receipts and Statements*

If you were to check your grocery or store receipt, approximately 50% of the time you would find an overcharge. This happens all the time and in some cases, the charge can be substantial. The same is true for credit card statements, bank statements, phone bills, etc. Check the detail because it is quite common to find errors. These mistakes can easily be corrected simply by asking and providing a copy of the receipt or statement.

70. *Challenge the Doctor/Hospital*

If you have stayed in the hospital recently, you know the outrageous charges associated with every thing used. While you could buy a box of bandages for a small cut in the drug store for $5.00, at the hospital, they will charge you $10 for one bandage. While the government and insurance companies are cracking down on these charges, you should check things closely and challenge anything that is ridiculously priced. The same is true for your doctor. One woman having a hysterectomy was asked by her doctor if she wanted her appendix removed at the same time. The patient thought it was a good idea and agreed. However, after the surgery when the bill came, there was an additional $1,200 for the removal of the appendix although the doctor never mentioned an extra charge. The woman called her doctor to discuss and the doctor removed the charge. If something seems way out of balance, question it. Something else that most people do not know about is what is called "professional courtesy." If you are having financial difficulties, you can ask your doctor if they will write off any balance owed as a professional courtesy. Many will and if not the full amount, at least some.

71. *Overdraft Protection*

Almost everyone has at one point or another had an insufficient check. Most banks charge $20 per returned check, which if not careful with your account, can quickly add up to a lot of money. If you have a savings account, consider adding overdraft protection onto your checking account so if you ever go into a negative balance, the money would automatically be covered by your savings. Most banks offer this service free.

72. *Bank Accounts*

Make sure you work with a qualified banker that can set up the "right" kind of account for your type of spending. There are numerous options specifically designed for people that write a good number of checks versus those who do not. Check with your existing bank to ensure you have what you really need and if they are not willing to work with you, change banks. In general, credit unions are good options. Their rates are typically lower and because they are employee owned, you can find better options.

73. *Organization*

You may be wondering what being organized has to do with saving money but in reality, it has a lot to do with it. For example, if you miss a credit card due date by one day, you will be charged anywhere from a 15% to 25% penalty. The same would be true for taxes. Missing one simple date can cost thousands. You need to be organized so you know the exact dates your bills are due as well as keep all receipts, contracts, etc. in an orderly manner.

74. *Good Health*

You need to make sure you take care of yourself physically. Missed dental cleanings (every six months) can lead to gum disease or tooth decay that can cost thousands to fix. The same is true for your health. After trying home remedies or over the counter medications, if you still do not feel well, see a doctor. It is far better to pay the doctor visit than to let your simple summer cold turn into pneumonia.

75. *Automobile Care*

Keep your car oil changed, tires rotated, and overall care up-to-date. First, the $30 for your oil change will save wear and tear on your car, which could result in significant money. Second, you need your car to get to and from work. By not having your car in top working condition could put you in a bad position when it comes to required transportation.

76. *Vacations*

While Paris, England, or Germany offers excitement, they also cost money to visit. Unfortunately, people on a regular basis forget about the United States and even the very state in which they live. One man had lived in Arizona his entire life. At age 50, when asked by a friend what the Grand Canyon was like, he was unable to answer because he had never been there. The next time you get ready to plan your family vacation, look around where you live and consider an exciting road trip that will not only be educating but cost effective. A vacation does not have to be expensive to be fun and memorable.

77. *Annual Maintenance*

Make a list of all annual maintenance items for your home such as air conditioner, heater, hot water heater, etc. Once again, being prepared and working in a proactive manner can save you unnecessary expenses. If you take care of your air conditioner by getting an annual tune up then you lower the risk of something going wrong during the hot summer months when it will be quite costly to repair.

78. *Borrowing Money*

Unless you have an emergency, avoid those enticing advertisements to lend you money at incredible rates. Banks and lending institutions make it much too easy to borrow money and especially during the holidays, they flash all their great advertisements drawing people in. Afterwards, you have borrowed money that you could have done without and now you are locked into a five-year repayment contract. If you want a new car or boat, it is better to save. If you do need a new car, avoid brand new cars, which lose massive amounts of appreciation the minute you drive off the lot. Instead, look for something a year or two old where you will still have a nice car but much more in line with an appropriate cost.

79. *Repair versus Replace*

Instead of spending $1,000 on that beautiful new couch, you might consider one of two options. If your couch frame is still good, you might spend $300 to have it recovered or purchase a quality slipcover for $100. Your couch will look brand new for much ess, than it would to replace. Another example would be if you have a lamp that you want to replace. Consider painting it and adding a new shade rather than spending money to buy a brand new one. Perhaps you have a washer, dryer, or refrigerator that is running a little sluggish. Find out the cost of repair over that of purchasing a new one. Even if you have an appliance with the wrong color, businesses offer fantastic paint jobs. With a little creativity, you will be amazed at how much can be repaired, thus saving you money.

80. *Dining Out*

Eating out can be expensive. Rather than stop eating out, simply cut back and look for options of two-for-one. Restaurants of all calibers offer weekly specials and if you check in your Sunday paper, you can often find special bargains. You might even think about signing up as a Mystery Shopper on the Internet where you can eat at fine restaurants free or at a huge discount just for writing a report on the food, service, and cleanliness.

81. *Plan Menus*

Although it will take some time initially, after you have planned a week's menu once, it will become much easier and best of all, it will save you money. Knowing exactly what you will be making helps you to shop for foods that can be used more than once. As an example, if you are going to have spaghetti on Tuesday, you could buy bulk ground beef at a better price and then use the other half for tacos on Saturday. Another option would be buying round steak where one night you fix Salisbury steak and then a few days later, you use the leftovers for breakfast hash. This will help you stretch meals and avoid last minute or impulse buying.

82. *Coordinate Efforts*

If you are married, make sure you and your spouse are working on the same agenda. If one is trying to save money while the other is busy spending, what is the point? When you work as a team, you can encourage each other to keep on track with your saving.

83. *Computer Software*

In order to keep on track with your debts and credits, you need to use some type of software such as Quicken or Quick Books. This will keep you focused on your goals and tasks while you strive to achieve them. Additionally, rather than buy software programs to download, first check Download.com or Freeware.com to see if there are free versions to download.

84. *Life Satisfaction*

Learn how to enjoy life and nature rather than possessions. The next time you feel like spending money, head to your local park where you can enjoy the warm sun, green grass, and towering trees without spending a dime. Being happy in life is far better than buying item after item. Having an inner peace is better than having a house filled with "things." That does not mean you cannot enjoy some of the finer things in life it just means learning how to be happy with yourself and not "things."

85. *Live Within your Means*

The quickest way to get in debt is to live beyond your means. Sure, most people want more than they have but life is not all about spending money. Be thankful for what you do have and learn how to enjoy the financial position you are in. This is where your budget will help identify the amount of money coming in against the amount of debt going out.

86. *Appropriate Deductions*

Rather than spending money just for the sake of spending, change the amount of deductions you have taken from your paycheck for your 401K or stock options. This is especially great if your company offers a competitive matching program. Increasing the amount you have deducted can quickly add up to a nice savings and is especially nice for retirement.

87. *Christmas Fund*

Many banks and financial institutions offer a Christmas Fund program. This is an excellent way to put aside some money for your holiday shopping so you do not end up with a ton of spending. With these programs, you do not even miss the money and better yet, less stress around the holidays.

88. *Previously Viewed*

Home videos and DVDs are hot items and perfect for any family entertainment. Now you can visit the major video chains and purchase previously viewed videos and DVDs for about half the cost. For example, at Blockbuster, you can purchase either one and get a 30-day warranty. This is still a wonderful way to have quality entertainment for a terrific savings. Another great option is to record your own movies either from TV or any of the popular cable channels such as HBO, Showtime or Disney. Rather than hitting the theater every weekend, make it a special occasion. Instead, pop your popcorn, grab a soda, spread out a blanket, and create your own theater-type atmosphere.

89. *Dinner Guests*

Invite friends over for dinner as a potluck. People love sharing their favorite recipe and by splitting dinner, everyone enjoys variety while saving money. In fact, make this a tradition amongst your friends.

90. *Instant Messaging / Microphone*

Rather than spend a small fortune in long distance, contact friends and family via instant messaging on the Internet. In addition, you can download a program that will allow you to connect a microphone and actually have a voice conversation free. All you pay for is the normal price of your Internet connection, which generally runs from $9.95 to $21.95 a month. Either option allows you to have real-time conversations for no extra money.

91. *Long Distance Calling*

If you do plan to use long-distance calling, shop around for the right carrier and be sure to read the small print. Even if you like your current carrier, you might be able to find an equally liked carrier for less money. Long distance is a very competitive market so deals are easy to find. The same would be true for your wireless carrier. The plans range vastly from one carrier to another so check out all your options for the best one. Do not forget to look at the coverage area. If you choose a carrier that does not have the right coverage for your area, even if the price is better, there is no savings if you cannot send or receive calls.

92. *Freeze Foods*

When you grocery shop, look for bargains on items that can be frozen. Most people do not even think about shredding block cheese and freezing it. Did you know that you could even freeze eggs? You can as long as you give them a little room to expand. When ready to use, simply set them out at room temperature. If you find apples on sale, make your own apple pies and freeze them or make applesauce. Many food items can be frozen with no problem.

Therefore, the next time you see a great bargain think about freezing. (Dairy products other than cheese do not generally freeze well).

93. *Ball Games*

Instead of spending your money on overpriced items at the ballgame, take your own cooler of food. Some professional stadiums no longer allow this so check before going. If you have a son or daughter that plays little league or soccer, this is a great way to save money over paying high concession stand prices.

94. *Discount Books*

Purchase a discount coupon book, which generally costs around $25. As long as you use it faithfully and base your choices on options featured in the book, you can save hundreds of dollars. These books are great for restaurants, hotels, car rentals, and tons of entertainment and provide great variety and even better discounts.

95. *Baby Food*

Instead of buying expensive baby food, make your own. You can use fresh vegetables such as peas, green beans, or corn, run it through the blender, and then freeze individual servings in ice cube trays. When it comes time to feed the baby, simply pop out a cube of food, defrost, and you have instant food. This is a real time and money saver. Most foods can be frozen. In fact, if you make family foods like spaghetti or soups simply make a smaller portion with less salt and spice, puree, freeze just like the vegetables.

96. *Squelch the Smoking*

This is probably the hardest habit to break but in addition to saving your health, you will also save money. Cigarettes have become quite expensive and if you car quit smoking, you will enjoy breathing easier and having more to put away for a rainy day.

97. _Rebate Programs_

When you shop, always keep your eyes open for rebate programs. Although filling out the forms and clipping the UPC codes from a box is a hassle, the money you save is worth it. Some rebate items are not listed as offering a rebate. Check out AsmartShop.com or Rebateplace.com to see if any of your recent purchases offer a rebate.

98. _Seasonal Buys_

One to three days after a holiday, stores mark their holiday items from 50% to 75% off. This is an ideal way to stock up on next year's Christmas or Halloween decorations. This is true for stores that sell seasonal clothing as well. Shopping for jackets or sweaters in the summer will provide you with great deals.

99. _Pocket Change_

Keep a jar or some type of container handy and each time you come home, drop in your change. Every time you break a bill, put the change in your container. You will be amazed how quickly your money will build.

100. _Freebies_

Check out freebie sites such as TotallyFreebies.com or SassySue.com where you will find all types of sample items ranging from cosmetics to books to clothing. Most have no shipping charges and the ones that do are minimal. By filling out a few forms, you will receive sample size soaps, lotions, shampoos and conditioners, etc., which are ideal for the traveler.

101. _See your Successes_

It is important to have an understanding of money. Keep a journal where you can see your successes when it comes to saving money. This is a difficult task and takes time to learn but worth it. By keeping a list of the situations or ways you have saved money in front of you, you will be encouraged to keep going. These successes can be small or large. For example, if you normally buy your lunch, costing you from $5.00 to $7.00 per day and one week straight you packed your own lunch for $3.00 per day that is a success. If you wanted to buy a new dress but held off until it went on sale, saving 50%, that is another success.

Saving money requires some investigative skills, desire, determination, and creativity. Once you get in the habit of saving money, you will feel better about yourself and enjoy life much more without debt hanging over your head!

Part 2 - 101 Ways To Create Huge Success In Life and Business

Most people want to be successful in life. There are goals set and then the hard work begins to reach those goals. The question is what is success? Actually, success can mean different things to different people.

For example, a person that owns their own oil changing service for vehicles might set their level of success at servicing 50 cars a day while someone who loves music might consider success as cutting their own CD. In addition, success does not always have to involve money. Success could be getting a good grade in a difficult class or learning how to bake the perfect chocolate cake.

Success comes in all different shapes and sizes with one common denominator. Success is important and it takes work to reach.

Regardless of what your specific success is, there are ways to surpass your goal. We have put together 101 tips that can be used for any success. These are ways to better yourself as a person, proven methods you can apply to reach success.

102. *Realize your Potential*

In order to succeed at anything, you need to see that you have the potential to reach your goals. For example, if you want to be a recording artist but have no singing ability, having success in this field is not likely. However, if you love working on cars and have a real talent for fixing engines and transmissions, and to you, success would mean working for NASCAR, you have potential to learn and achieve that success.

103. *Don't Look Back*

Everyone has failures or mistakes from the past. To have success, you need to learn from your past and value those difficult lessons but do not every dwell on the past. Simply move forward and make better, more educated decisions from the lessons learned.

104. *Dare to Dream*

To succeed, you need to have dreams and aspirations. Be honest with yourself as to what you want out of life and what you want to give of your life. Allow your mind to dream and think big.

105. *Business Plan*

Create a Business Plan as your very first step if you are planning to build a business. Whether you will be searching for investors or not, this plan will be the blueprint to your success. The Business Plan will consist of market trends, financial planning, competitive analysis, exit strategies, marketing and promotional options, everything about your goal. When going before an investor, you will be required to have a Business Plan. This is by far the most important document of all. If your success were something personal, you would not need to create a Business Plan although a project plan would be a good option to allow you to keep track of everything involving your goal.

106. *Don't Give Up*

To reach success, you have to persevere. Even Thomas Edison had to learn this. When he was creating the incandescent light bulb, it took him more than 10,000 times to get it right. Keep striving even when it becomes challenging.

107. *Have an Unstoppable Attitude*

You need to have determination. With good intentions, there may be a close friend or family member that feels it would be better if you focused your attention in another direction. Uphold your unstoppable attitude, determined to succeed.

108. *Stop the Complaining*

You might think there is no correlation between complaining and success when in fact there is a connection. When you are spending time complaining about the obstacles you are facing, you are wasting so much time being negative that you are actually loosing chances to move forward. Instead of thinking of challenges as problems, think of them as opportunities.

109. *Focus on Something you Like*

To increase your chance of succeeding, you should concentrate your efforts on something you enjoy. When you start out, make a list of everything you find interesting. Then in a second column, write down the skills you have in relation to each of those items. This will help you narrow choices down based on interest and skill, which gets you started in the right direction for success.

110. *Change your Circumstances*

You have a choice in life to accept your position or change it. If you choose to plug along in life hoping that something will change for the better, you will not get very far. Always remember that when it comes to changing your circumstances, you can – you have that power. As an example, women who are in abusive situations often feel controlled and powerless to get out of the situation. They have the same choice of changing their circumstances as you do. If your circumstances lower the chances of success, you need to change them.

111. *Have a Plan*

Even if it is flimsy to begin with, you should construct a plan to include goal, milestones, deliverables such as contracts, business plans, etc., and accomplishments. This will provide you with a visual as to what you are working for, what milestones you have successfully met, and where you need to do better.

112. _Accept Responsibility_

You need to accept responsibility if you make a bad decision or fall behind in your plan. Let us say that you have set some firm milestones that need to be accomplished in order for you to move to the next step. However, you got tired of working hard and took some time to play, which is fine as long as it does not affect your goals. Now months have passed and you are way behind schedule. This delay has closed several doors of opportunities. Who is to blame?

113. _Be Happy_

A positive mind and happy, upbeat attitude will help you succeed. It has been proven in many studies that a person living in a happy state generally gets much further in just about everything they do. This relates to attitude. Just as bad attitude can pull you down, good attitude and a happy, healthy mind will help you meet your objectives.

114. _No Shortcuts_

An old cliché states, "Anything worth doing is worth doing well." This should be your motto. When you want to succeed, you cannot afford to take shortcuts. Taking shortcuts leads to imperfection and inadequacies. Always strive for the best, even if it requires a little more time and effort.

115. _Have Courage_

Depending on what your specific success is, it may take courage to arrive at your desired destination. For example, if you have a dream of being a writer and to you, that is success, but according to your long line of family members who have all gone on to be doctors, the only success in their minds is if you follow down the medical path. This means you will have to have courage to stand up for what you believe and desire to do, even if it means disappointing family.

116. *Be Excited to Learn*

Referring back to the analogy of Edison, when asked about his failures by a young boy, Edison commented, "Young man, I didn't fail 9,999 times, I discovered 9,999 ways not to invent the light bulb." As you work toward your specific success, always enjoy opportunities to learn, even if it takes longer than you think it should.

117. *Share your Success*

Although this may be more at the end of the process, it is important. When you finally do reach your success, use your experience to teach, guide, and mentor others so that they too might succeed.

118. *Seek Input*

Whatever your idea of success, conduct a "sanity check" throughout the process of reaching your goal. This should be done with someone you trust and who is themselves successful. Ask them to provide honest feedback about your success and as you move through different milestones, bounce concerns or new ideas off them to help keep you on the right track.

119. *Toxic Poisoning*

No, we are not talking about actual poison but toxic people that can poison. Unfortunately, it would be great if close friends or co-workers could share in your success but all too often, there will be someone who is either dealing with the "green monster" of jealousy or has a case of the "I knew that" syndrome. If you are serious about reaching your goal and being successful, you will need to rid your life of these people. While you may not be able to get them out of your life completely, you should avoid them as best as possible. If this is a person, you see every day, keep your goals to yourself, and avoid that specific subject.

120. *Be a Good Listener*

To succeed, you need to learn how to listen first. Pay attention to other people who have enjoyed successes in their life, attend seminars given by people that can motivate and encourage, or be open to hearing that a particular idea is not a good one. Good listening takes time to learn but in the end, it will be your greatest tool.

121. *Birds of a Feather*

If you have a goal of being a best-selling author, find friends and mentors who either have achieved that same goal or are also pursuing a successful writing career. It is important to surround yourself with people that can associate with your goal and passion, people who understand the burning desire to succeed and can encourage when you meet with disappointments.

122. *Little Red Engine*

Do you remember the story of the caboose that was desperately trying to make it over a very large hill? He kept telling himself repeatedly, "I think I can, I think I can." When you start feeling overwhelmed or defeated, tell yourself aloud these same words. While it may seem a little awkward at first, stand in front of a mirror and tell yourself, "I think I can, I think I can." You might even change the words to, "I know I can!"

123. *Be Proactive*

While it may take time to learn how to identify ways to avoid obstacles or failures, get into the habit of tackling problems before they arise. This will help you avoid wasting precious time on your road to success.

124. *Stay Motivated*

When striving for the big goal of success, it is critical to stay motivated. Find inspiring and motivational tapes, seminars, books, movies; whatever you are able to get your hands on. When you start to feel a little down and out and doubt starts to creep in, turn to these motivational tools to help you keep on track. A few excellent motivators include Tony Robbins, Norman Vincent Peale, Jim Rohn, Zig Ziglar, and Les Brown.

125. _Give Yourself a Break_

While being determined is important, do not be so hard on yourself that you become critical of every move you make. Give yourself some room to make mistakes and be flexible with you. That does not mean you can miss goals but it does mean that if you do, you find out how to avoid that from happening again and then get back to business.

126. _Be Passionate_

Fall in love with what your success. Okay, although that sounds funny, you need to have an intimate passion with your interest. You can do this regardless of what your success is. By having passion for what you are doing and driving toward, you will automatically put more effort into it. Passion is a good thing as long as it does not become an obsession.

127. _Don't Settle_

If you have a goal of becoming a world-famous chef and you know you have both desire and skill, do not just settle to become a short order cook at your local family-style restaurant. While that may be good training ground, do not allow yourself to lose sight of your ultimate goal.

128. _No Excuses_

Many famous actors, music artists, inventors, etc., had special challenges ranging from learning disabilities to physical disabilities. Take Beethoven for example. He was born deaf yet he went on to be one of the world's greatest composers or Joni Erickson who was paralyzed from the neck down yet she learned to paint with her mouth. Today, her paintings are famous around the world and worth millions. If you are faced with a special challenge of your own, while you may have to adjust things from time to time, do not use excuses. If you want something bad enough, there is a way!

129. *Getting Past Fear of Failure*

Being afraid of failure is a normal emotion for every person on the planet. How you get past that fear is the determining factor between failing and succeeding. You can do that by setting realistic goals and then examining those goals on occasion to do any necessary realignment. Above all, believe in yourself and the desire burning within.

130. *Patience and Dues*

Succeeding takes time. A goal worth setting will take time to achieve. Be patient with yourself, the people around you, and the process it takes to become successful, also referred to as "paying your dues." Just like the chef scenario, it takes time to be a master chef. Pay your dues by learning and working your way up the ladder to success.

131. *Good Time / Resource Management*

Being successful also means keeping to a schedule. In addition, you need to learn how much is too much. Good time and resource management will help you ensure that you use your time wisely and that you are not adding third portions onto a plate still overflowing with seconds.

132. *Make Opportunities*

Rather than wait for opportunity to find you, you need to find opportunities. This might be watching for business opportunities in the paper regarding small businesses being sold, great real estate opportunities, and investments with stocks, bonds, or mutual funds, taking a talent and turning it into an entrepreneurial adventure. People that have reached financial status will tell you that they look for ways to seize opportunities, not wait for opportunities to come knocking on their door because it will not happen that way.

133. *Attitude*

Putting yourself in the right attitude for success should be at the top of your list. Staying positive and surrounding yourself with friends, that share a positive attitude will help you succeed. Do not allow negative thoughts to slip into your mind. Attend motivational seminars and find ways to enjoy life. A good attitude will allow you to turn any bad situation into a learning experience. You have heard the saying, "The glass is either half-full or half-empty." You need to adopt the attitude that life is half-full. The result is that you will feel better, have more energy, and have a much higher opportunity for success.

134. *Be Thankful*

You need to be thankful for not only your accomplishments but also your failures. Having a grateful attitude is important. It will help you stay humble, which in turn, will help you continue striving for the ultimate in success.

135. *Keep a Journal*

As you work hard to reach success, regardless of what you consider that success to be, you need to be able to see your accomplishments. Start a journal and track every thing you have conquered. When you feel discouraged or frustrated, reflect on what you have achieved, and rejuvenate yourself.

136. *Rewards*

When children do something great, parents will reward them with something nice, whether a kind word of encouragement or a new toy. When people do well in their job, they get raises. As you surpass your milestones, reward yourself. Treat yourself to something nice – a new dress, a new fishing pole, whatever you like, be sure to award yourself for a job well done.

137. _Watch for Scams_

Whether you are just starting out or expanding an existing business, unfortunately, there are thousands of people waiting to defraud you out of money. If something appears too good to be true – IT IS! Always conduct thorough research and never jump into opportunities that look perfect. If someone becomes pushy, wanting you to make a quick decision on any type of investment, do not walk away – RUN away!

138. _Focus on the Big Picture_

As you make your way toward success, you will be challenged with big obstacles as well as small obstacles. Pick your battles wisely. While you need to resolve the small issues, do not dwell on them and lose precious time and energy when you should be focusing on the bigger picture. In other words, do not allow the menial things to clutter your mind and monopolize your time.

139. _Make the Best of Each Day_

Try to live every day as though it were your last. Make the most of every day and accomplish something. Even if it is something small, every baby step adds up to a huge success in the end.

140. _Make the Process and Adventure_

You should look at every angle of your journey as an exciting adventure. When you think of your childhood years, you loved investigating the unknown. Carry this with you as you strive toward success. Anticipate the excitement of each accomplishment – make it a real adventure.

141. _Don't Neglect Things_

Especially when things are small and do not appear to have a major impact on the big picture, you need to ensure you follow through and complete your tasks. Those little things can quickly add up to a big mess if not taken care of in a timely and efficient manner.

142. *Offer Praise*

If you have people helping you out, whether on a volunteer basis or a full-time employee, always offer praise. These people are an important part of your success and by providing praise and support; in return, they will show dedication and work hard to help you reach your goal.

143. *Set Daily Goals*

In order to visualize your accomplishments and stay encouraged, you need to set daily goals. These goals can be as simply as a follow up phone call or a written letter to an investor. Whatever the task is, get it done. In addition to keeping the process for your success on track, it will help you to feel like you are making accomplishments, pushing you closer and closer to the success.

144. *Collaborate with Others*

More than likely, you will reach various times when you do not have the appropriate expertise to accomplish something. This is the time collaboration and/or networking is valuable. These relationships can help you answer questions, provide guidance, and provide the ongoing support and encouragement you will need.

145. *Customer Relations*

Keep your line of communication open with your customers. If they have a problem, show them the deserved respect and resolve the issue quickly. Make occasional phone calls to see if they have any needs. This will let your customers know that you are there for them and care about their business. This relationship is what is going to keep you on the road to success. After all, the customer is your link between failure and success.

146. *Repositioning and Reflection*

On occasion, reflect on what you have accomplished as well as your open milestones and ensure you are still heading in the right direction. Repositioning along the way to success is perfectly normal and to be expected. You may have been struggling with something specific. Rather than continue battling this issue, reflect on what has not been working, and reposition yourself so you do not have to keep battling the same things repeatedly.

147. *Accept Responsibility*

You and you alone are responsible for your success. While you will have help in many instances, the bottom line is that you are responsible. You need to be surrounded by the right people, working with the right investors, going about meeting your success in the right way. It is you that will make the choices and therefore, your responsibility to make the right choices. In other words, your desire for success must always be greater that any obstacle that stands in your way.

148. *Community*

Regardless of what your goal for success is, get involved with your community. First, get involved with town meetings, the local Chamber of Commerce, and attend community functions. You will be amazed at the opportunities for support, business ideas, and financing available right there in your own neighborhood.

149. *Record Keeping*

Always keep your records up to date. This would include contact information, investor information, Business Plans, attorney information, accounting, everything you touch regarding your goal. In addition, keep your files on your computer backed up and current. First, you never know when you are going to be asked for a specific document and need to provide quick turn-around.

Second, computers do crash and it would be a disaster if all of your information were suddenly gone.

150. *Get out of Debt*

Take time to get any debts paid off, especially credit card debts that will cost you a fortune in interest. This is especially important if you will be seeking funding as a part of your particular success. You want to ensure that your records and credit are clean if you need to make a presentation before an investor, asking for money.

151. *Read*

Stay current on the industry news that your goal falls in. Learn about current trends, company failures or successes, new ideas; whatever information you can find. For example, if you have decided to open a retail store and have a great idea and a real passion for your goal, read about that specific type of store, location, potential revenue, downfalls, everything. This information will be a part of your business plan and is crucial.

152. *Location, Location, Location*

If you are planning to open a business, you have probably already heard how important the right location is in order to be successful. Do not settle for any location as a means of getting the doors of your business open. Instead, take the appropriate amount of time and find the "right" location. This will be one of the best decisions you can make. It would be far better to delay your opening a month in order to secure the right location than to open early in the wrong location!

153. *Good Habits*

Being successful, whether personal or business requires good habits. It is just like trying to do well in school. You have to have good study habits in order to do well on tests. It is the same for the business world. You need to do your "homework." Read the newspaper, scout out opportunities, and take time each day to dedicate specifically to your endeavor.

154. _Be Open to Improvement_

Sometimes, people get into the habit of thinking they have the answers needed. You need to accept that you do not have all the answers and more importantly, be open to recommendations from other people. That does not mean you have to agree or even follow those suggestions, but it does mean to listen. You never know when someone will have an idea that will make things easier and more functional, ultimately helping you arrive at your goal more efficiently.

155. _Take Notes_

How many times have you had an idea either through a dream, while doing the dishes, or sitting at your desk, and have thought that as soon as you have time, you will make a note of it. When that free time rolls around, you have forgotten some or all of that great idea. Keep a journal or notepad handy at all times. When you have an idea, write it down immediately.

156. _Take care of Yourself_

Being successful means taking care of you, both physically and emotionally. You will need to have energy, focus, and rest. In turn, this will help you concentrate and put in the hours required to be successful. Without taking proper care of yourself, you will end up struggling and your business could feel the effects.

157. _Take Good Notes_

Whether you are at a seminar, a casual meeting, or notice something special in the news, take good, comprehensive notes. This is not always a natural skill but something that has to be acquired. You want to pay attention to the emphasis being made capture it. Even if there are materials being handed out, if there is something that you feel you should capture separately, do it. Good notes will help you learn better and provide additional reference points.

158. *Participate*

If attending seminars or lectures that will help you get ahead, if there is the opportunity, participate by asking questions or making valid points. Participation is a great way to remember what is being taught.

159. *Be Serious*

Take your efforts to success seriously. Success is a serious thing and it takes serious dedication. You have to have the mindset that this is not going to be all play, at least not in the beginning.

160. *Study Time*

No matter what your goal for success, you should set aside some time to study. If you want to be a successful hair stylist, study different styles, colors, and trends. If you want to be a veterinarian, study animals. Whatever your success, take time to read, research, and ask many questions. You should also consider volunteering at the local beauty school or hair salon or your veterinarian's office. Ask if you can follow them around for a day or two and without getting in the way, observe, and ask questions.

161. *Apply What You Learn*

Since you will be setting milestones as you reach for your success, apply what you have learned through each phase of the process. Doing is a much more powerful tool than simply reading or watching.

162. *Provide Yourself Time*

You need to be sure to allow yourself some time just for pleasure. Being successful is hard work so to avoid burnout; you need to treat yourself to a night out or just time to sit back, watch TV, and do absolutely nothing once in awhile.

163. *Set Realistic Goals*

People wanting to be successful often want overnight results. Unfortunately, that is not going to happen. You need to do an analysis to determine a realistic amount of time it will take to reach your specific success. As you go through your Business Plan you may find times that dates have to adjusted but even if there are changes, keep it realistic. Otherwise, you will become frustrated and quit!

164. *Talk About It*

Talking about your goals for success not only keeps it in the front of your mind but also keeps up your excitement level. In addition, it adds in an element of accountability. Think about it, you go around telling everyone that you are going to be a masseuse, those people are going to be expecting, and anxious to see you succeed. By talking about your goals, you are creating a motivational system – a system of accountability.

165. *Don't Make Quick Decisions*

When things in your plan need to change, unless necessary, do not make quick decisions. Just as it took time to plan in the beginning, it will take time to change. You want to make sure you are making the right decisions when changes come up. Do your research just as you did in the beginning and then make educated choices.

166. *Avoid Stress*

When you strive to be successful, stress is a natural part of the process. Do everything you can to avoid stress. Adding in unnecessary stress into the equation will take focus away from accomplishing your goals. You can listen to relaxing tapes, get a professional massage, take a walk, or whatever helps you to relax. When you start feeling overwhelmed, stop, change direction, and avoid stress. The only thing stress accomplishes is draining your think power and creativity.

167. *Learn How to Delegate*

As you start getting closer to your goal of success, you will find that there are many more things to do than hours in the day. If going into business, consider hiring someone; even part-time or on a freelance basis to help take some of your load. If your success is more on a personal basis, have family or friends pitch in to help you get things done. You will be amazed at how much this will help ease the situation and allow you the proper amount of time to focus on the things that need your full attention.

168. *Be a Problem Solver*

Rather than stew over things or let stress overtake you, find ways to become a problem solver. Look at ways that you might find new customers, increase productivity, or resolve issues.

169. *Conduct Research*

It is important to know what you are getting into. First, you will want to conduct research as far as the business, industry, or interest associated with your particular success. Second, the research will help you stay up to date on trends, which may or may not require you to make adjustments in your own goal. For example, if you were interested in opening a particular business focusing on a specific technology and that technology took a turn to another direction, new advancements, you may need to change the direction you were going for your own business. Unless you kept up on research, you would not know when a change was needed and therefore, would end up building a business already headed for failure.

170. *Offer a Guarantee*

If you have created a business that offers either products or services, in order to get and keep customers coming back, they have to know that you stand behind what you offer. Providing a guarantee will help your business grow and reach the highest level of success.

171. *Get Excited*

Do you remember your first trip to see a professional baseball game and how exciting it was to see the thousands of people cheering, enjoying the mouthwatering smell of popcorn and hot dogs, and hoping that you might get a chance to catch a foul ball? Perhaps you can remember your first prom, being excited that the right boy asked you to the dance, shopping for the perfect glamour dress, and buying your date a corsage. You need to be excited about your venture for success. Remember some of the things that brought true excitement to your heart when you were growing up and add that same excitement to your grownup life.

172. *Expand your Mind*

Whatever your idea of success, take it one-step further. Stretch your mind and reach just one-step higher than you thought you could reach. If you were going to open an ice cream store, offering 30 flavors, go one more step and make it 31. Okay, you get the idea.

173. *Be a Strong Leader*

Learn to be a good leader and a good mentor. Enjoy making a difference and in guiding others to achieve their potential as well. Help people reach to new horizons.

174. *Be Logical*

Okay, you may be thinking that logic itself is logical. However, being logic in many cases means having some level of analytical ability. Regardless of the way you think, find the logic in it. This will help you think and plan clearly and honestly.

175. _Give 100% Effort_

If you are going to succeed, you have to be able to get through tough times. You will have to rise to challenges and not quit. You have to plan to go the extra mile and make personal sacrifices. Succeeding means giving 100% effort. Stay focused while keeping your performance on a consistent basis.

176. _Take Classes_

Take some classes at college where you can get a certification. Enhancing yourself on a personal level will boost everything about you, making you feel better, about the person you are. When you feel better, you achieve more. This is a great time to obtain your certification in CPR, First Aid, a computer class, or some other outside interest you have.

177. _Understand your Goal_

A great challenge is to prove to yourself that you can do it. One of the ways to prove this to you is to take on responsibility. If your goal for success involves opening a restaurant, work in a restaurant as a server to get a perspective of all the jobs involved to make the restaurant a success. Understand the entire business from the ground up.

178. _Raise your Standards_

You may think you are working your tail off and you probably are. Try raising the bar just a little bit. Always expect the best from yourself. Do not beat yourself up if you do not always hit 100% but increase your standards and strive for more.

179. _Unconscious Power_

The unconscious mind is a very powerful tool. Take advantage of this and each night before heading off to bed, take some time to pose questions to yourself and then allow your mind to hash them out while you sleep. In addition, mediate in whatever way you find relaxing before going to bed to clear your mind from clutter and allow the subconscious mind to go to work.

180. *Paint a Picture*

A great way to keep working toward your goal is to see it. If you want to open a computer store, find a picture or article about Bill Gates when he first got started. If your success is to lose weight, go to Diets.com or Slimfast.com and print off a before and after picture of someone that has a similar body type to yourself. Perhaps your goal is to redecorate your bedroom. Again, locate before and after pictures on the Internet of decorated rooms. Seeing is believing!

181. *Develop Uniformity*

At first, this may be a little challenging but strive to keep things on an even keel. This will keep your efforts and focus from going up and down. The more you can stay the course the quicker you will reach your goal to success.

182. *Just Do It*

Okay, so Nike coined that phrase but it is so accurate. Quit putting things off and just do it. If you want it bad enough, go for it!

183. *Identify Procrastinations*

If you have a problem with procrastination, make a list of the things you constantly put on hold. This will help you identify your poor patterns and make the appropriate adjustments. Local colleges often have improvement courses regarding making better decisions and procrastination. Locate a class that would help you with this kind of challenge.

184. *Want Versus Need*

When you strive for success, do it because you *want* it, not because you *need* it. When you want something, it brings about intention, desire, and action. However, when you need something, it will lead to pain, stress, and frustration.

185. *Be Independent*

Do not be afraid to go for what you know is the right thing for you. Being independent allows you to take control over your destiny and emotional state. Stand firm in what you believe and do not allow other people to determine how you feel or what you believe in.

186. *Economic Value*

Considering your talent, also look at things that can help create economic value. These types of goals have better chance of being successful and lasting. Is there something in your community that could bring about more revenue? As an example, do you live in a smaller town where there are no fast food restaurants, causing people to drive miles outside of your town for a cheeseburger and shake? If so, perhaps opening a small fast food restaurant would be a great option. You could have the success of running your own business while bringing something to your community.

187. *Learn a New Skill*

Learn new skills that will enhance your success. If you want to become a hairstylist and someday open a line of salons, in addition to cutting hair, learn how to braid, color, do weaves, etc.

188. *Appreciate Life*

Do not burn any bridges in life. Appreciate life, people, everything around you. Learn as much as you can from every person you meet. Do not turn people away just because you do not agree with them. You never know, the very people you turn away may be the very people that come to your rescue during a time of difficulty.

189. _The Right Marketing_

When you get ready to start marketing your business or idea, never rely on one method of marketing. It is important to look at several options since nothing will last forever.

190. _Believe_

Not only do you need to believe in the product or service you are building to success, you also need to believe in you. Your confidence is what will get you through the difficult challenges and build credibility with your customers.

191. _Know your Customers_

You should know, really know, your customers, especially your top ten. Find out what they like and dislike. What other products or services would be of value to them? These very relationships are what will keep your business going. It is crucial to consider your customer's desires all of the time.

192. _Plan your Costs_

Unbelievably, there are thousands of entrepreneurs that start a business without the foggiest idea of what their costs are going to be. Either there is an estimation that is way overstated or understated. From the very beginning, you need to have a strong handle on knowing what you will need to get your business started and keep it running. Additionally, you need to have projections for your future success. Know your numbers and make sure they are accurate.

193. _Timing is Everything_

You have probably heard it before – timing is everything. Especially when it comes to opening a business, there is a right and a wrong time to start a business. This would be extremely important if your business has cycles or is seasonal. For example, if you are starting a business to do landscaping, the winter months when snow is on the ground is not the right time. You can be working toward your Business Plan, marketing ideas, finding investors, if required, etc., during those cold months, but you certainly would not want to open your doors for the first time in the heart of winter.

194. *Keep it Lean*

Start-up businesses do not have room for "dead" weight. As an example, when first starting out, if you need some assistance, rather then hiring a permanent employee that will involve salary, insurance, other benefits, etc., consider a temporary employee until the business grows. Keep improving the bottom line before you start adding on more expenses to your business.

195. *Get the Word Out*

If your success is focused on a business, when you get ready to open your doors, make sure you get the message out. This will include marketing promotions, advertising, sending out a press release, etc. The more people know about your business, the better chance of you have of reaching success.

196. *Guard your Emotions*

Keeping emotions in check is not always an easy task. You will have times of disappointment that will require you to react with integrity. You may feel like crying and feel as though your world has just ended. Keep telling yourself that it has not ended and you will just have to make some adjustments in your plan. Never allow anger to be a response. You never know the trickle down effect of that anger and how it could permanently damage your reputation.

197. *Be Nice*

Study after study has shown that people with pleasing personalities have an easier time reaching success. Now only are they more levelheaded in handling the business but they also draw people around them that are eager and willing to help. In fact, in addition to being pleasing, be polite, show true interest, and have a great sense of humor.

198. *Break Bad Habits*

Habits, regardless of size or nature, can be exceptionally difficult to break. This will take a lot of effort but you can do it. Unfortunately, poor habits can be the one aspect of your behavior that could be the obstacle to your success. If you have a habit of sniffling or chewing your nails when you get nervous or saying demeaning or offensive things as a way of trying to control, to be successful, whether on a personal or business leve , you have to stop.

199. *Improve Efficiency*

You will want to develop your potential to its fullest. The more efficient you can become the better job you will do. Be efficient with your time by not procrastinating and efficient with your effort by staying focused.

200. *Have Balance in your Life*

Imagine yourself on a canoe with another person. The day is beautiful, sunny, and warm. The two of you are floating along without a care in the world. Suddenly, ripples of water start rocking the canoe and without proper balance, both of you, along with all your belongings, are thrown into the cold water. It is the same when you strive for success. You have to find balance not only for yourself but also for others around you. Balance means providing time away from work for pleasure, working extra hours when required, knowing when a new direction is required, etc.

201. *Have Fun*

When people start into the process of being successful, whether for personal growth or starting a business, they may start by incorporating fun, but within a very short time, they realize it is hard work and the fun simply falls by the wayside. If you look at some of the most successful people in the world such as Sam Walton, Oprah Winphrey, or Ross Perot, you will find common threads that run between all of them. First, they started with nothing; second, they are all multi-millionaires many times over, and third, they have fun. They enjoy life, the people around them, and even find enjoyment in the challenges. This one element is often forgotten. This is a crucial element for success and should be a part of your plan.

202. *Face your Weaknesses*

The best way to get better at anything and to be successful is to face the weaknesses we all possess. Everyone has weaknesses and in order to be better, think clear, act appropriately, and succeed, you have to identify the areas you need to improve on and then take action to turn your weaknesses into strengths.

There is no better gratification than being successful. Accept that you are in for some hard work but the results will be incredible. Use these tips as guidelines and step outside the box. Take action and succeed!

Part 3 - 101 Ways to Get in Better Shape and Stay That Way!

More than any other time in history, people are all vying to have the best, healthiest body possible. The health and fitness industries are making billions of dollars every year on herbal supplements, fitness equipment, gyms, and special diets. If you watch TV or read magazines, there is always some intriguing commercial asking for money to help you get into shape.

While many of these options are good and healthy, others you should stay as far away from as possible. Recently, a professional baseball player died at the age of 23. In his locker, a bottle was discovered containing Ephedrine. The FDA just issued a warning that people need to heed.

Now that you have made a commitment to take care of your body, both internal and external, it is critical to your overall health that you do it the right way. Here are some tips for both health and fitness that will help you lose weight, discover ways to maintain a better healthy lifestyle, and be in the best shape of your life – all the smart way!

For sake of clarity, we have broken this down into two categories. One for health, which focuses on herbal supplements, weight loss, dieting, rest, and everything you need to know about taking care of your body on the inside.

The other section is fitness, which has both internal and external benefits. One the outside, fitness includes weight lifting, running, sports, walking, things you can do to enhance, tone, and build muscle. However, fitness also has benefits for the inside such as great cardiovascular benefits among others.

HEALTH

First, we will start out with Health:

203. *Acupuncture*

The use of acupuncture dates back more than 2,000 years. This is a traditional medicine of Japan, China, and other Eastern countries. The use of acupuncture is beneficial in that it stimulates areas of the body that have a direct correlation to internal organs. By placing fine needles into specific points, the body is encouraged to promote natural healing, improve function, and provide an overall boost to your system. When these needles are inserted, they go into Meridians, which are channels somewhat like streams within the body. Just as there might be a boulder sitting in a stream blocking the flow of water, it can be the same for the channels of blood in your system. Acupuncture helps to remove these obstacles by providing stimulation, thus improving health.

204. *Biofeedback*

Biofeedback is a method used to help blood pressure, muscle tension, heart rates, brain activity, and other bodily functions. Basically, biofeedback is a painless system that is hooked up to your body and then through electrical signals received from tightening of your muscles, you would be able to receive those signals by a light telling you that you are tightening your muscles. This in turn trains you to be aware of when you are bringing on stress and to help you identify when you need to relax your body. Biofeedback is very successful and can be used for migraine headaches, chronic pain, high blood pressure, epilepsy, and much more, which can occur when you tense up.

205. *Therapeutic Massage*

You might be thinking what does getting a massage do for my health other than to make me feel good. Actually, therapeutic massage has many benefits. For example, it can help alleviate pain, reduce stress, and promote good health. When a person gets a therapeutic massage, they are actually getting the benefit of function improvement with circulatory, muscular, skeletal, nervous systems, lymphatic, and can even help the body heal after an illness or injury. Depending on what the specific health issue, there is a Swedish Massage, which is a more relaxing massage good for headaches, back stress, and muscle cramps, Pressure Point Therapy, helpful for some injuries as well as circulation problems, headache and muscle tension, insomnia, anxiety, and more. Finally, Sports Massage focuses on muscle groups used for different sports. Licensed masseuse can help with the issues mentioned as well as allergies, arthritis, asthma, carpal tunnel syndrome, depression, digestive disorders, myofascial pain, limited range of motion, sinusitis, and TMJ. The next time you tell someone you are going to get a massage, you can simply explain that it is for the benefit of your health.

206. *Eat Less Later in the Day*

Everyone knows, whether they want to admit it or not, reducing calories will help you to lose weight. However, just as you should reduce the calorie intake, you need to know when to eat. Breakfast is the most important meal of the day and the one meal that should not be missed. Lunch should be healthy but a less than what you ate for breakfast. As you approach dinner, eat healthy but light. Avoid after dinner snacks or eating before bed!

207. *Saucy but Healthy*

Eating bland foods is boring, unsatisfying, and if that is what your diet consists of, more than likely, you will be off it shortly after you start. If you enjoy good tasting food, some sauces and spices can enhance your food while not adding calories to your food. The next you grill meat, consider using one of these:

- Reduced-salt Soy Sauce
- Mustard
- Salsa
- Worcestershire Sauce
- Vinegar (this comes in wonderful flavors)
- Teriyaki Sauce
- Tomato Sauce
- Hot Sauce

208. _Supplements and Vitamins_

While some supplements and vitamins on the market are not worth buying and some, such as Ephedrine, have been proven dangerous, other sources are healthy. Most important, you need to understand what it is you are taking, and strictly follow dosage just as you would medication that has been prescribed. If you are unsure, check with your physician, a nutritionist, or a reputable health food store. Many supplements that are good for overall health include grape seed extract, Glucosamine, aloe vera, and Selenium. Vitamins to consider would include Vitamin E, Vitamin C, B-12, Iron, Magnesium, and Calcium.

209. _Eliminate Stress_

You have probably heard this before. Stress is a key contributor to poor health. Study after study has found that when a person is stressed, the body reacts. The result of stress could be high-blood pressure, tension headaches, upset stomachs, poor posture, and so on. Keeping stress in check will help you manage your overall health much better.

210. _ZZZZZZZZZZZ_

Does sleep really affect health? You bet it does. During sleep, your body is resting and recovering from all the work is has done throughout the day. Your serotonin levels are brought back in line, your muscles relax, and mind is allowed to clear itself in preparation for the next day. If you are not getting the proper amount of sleep, you will notice it in a physical way. While there is no magic number, usually between six and eight hours a night is appropriate. If you have difficulty getting to sleep, before you climb into bed, try Yoga, listening to soft, relaxing music, a glass of wine, or if you can talk someone into it, a good massage.

211. _Laugh it Off_

The medical field has proven that laughter actually works with your body toward good health. Have you ever heard the expression, "Laughter is the best medicine"? The truth is, when you laugh, several positive things happen. Your muscles relax; stress hormone product is reduced; you forget about pain; your body's immune system is improved; high-blood pressure is lowered; the heart and lungs are strengthened; and overall, you feel better!

212. *Nutrition*

People often confuse "dieting" with nutrition. Your body needs to have nutrients replaced, whether through foods being eaten or supplements. Do you remember what you learned in elementary school about the four major food groups? As adult, eating balanced meals from these groups still applies. It is important to remove the "junk food" from your diet and stick with healthy foods. If you do not like certain things such as fruits or vegetables, be sure you are taking a supplement to get the nutrients needed. Another consideration is if you are a vegetarian. There are certain benefits taken from meat such as iron and B-12 that you should consider taking a supplement for in exchange for the meat.

213. *Yoga*

The practice of Yoga is actually a spiritual practice. However, with the many benefits received it has quickly become a popular choice to thousands of people strictly for health. Yoga helps stretch out muscles and ligaments, tone the body, and the greatest benefit is that it helps to clear the mind. Having a clear mind works toward a healthy body.

214. *Stop Smoking*

You have probably heard this more times, than you can count but facts are facts! There is no other way to say it – smoking is not only bad for your health, it is deadly! One woman in her late thirties had smoked for 10 years. She had tried everything from watering down her cigarettes, throwing them away, wearing a patch, chewing gum, you name it, she tried it. She really wanted to quit but the addiction was so strong she was finding it impossible.

The mother of an 11-year old daughter and a 13-year old son, she was taken by surprise when something happened that made her quit smoking in one day. Her son told her that he had something very important to tell her. With a quick response of, "Okay, what is it?" he said, "No, I really need to talk to you." She knew by the look on his face and the tone of his voice that this was something important. Her son looked her square in the face and without wavering said, "I want you to quit smoking because I don't want you to die. I want a mother in my life." With that, she walked over to an ashtray, put out her cigarette, and now almost seven years later, she still does not smoke. While this will not work for everyone, the next time you pick up a cigarette; take a minute to consider how your child or family would feel if you were no longer around.

215. *Mixing Medications*

Many people do not realize how dangerous mixing medications can be. In fact, some combinations are lethal. If you are on medication, make sure your physician knows everything you take, including herbs and supplements. To take it one-step further, when you have a new prescription filled, ask the pharmacist if there are any bad interactions with your other current medication.

216. *Drink Wisely*

There is nothing wrong with a couple of social drinks or a glass of wine or beer with dinner, but if you drink, you need to be wise. First, if you drink to the point of being drunk, keep in mind that you are causing damage to your liver. Second, if you drink, NEVER drink and drive.

217. *Young at Heart*

Regardless of your age, if you start acting too old, you will actually not benefit yourself at all. Studies have shown that people who act old, feel old, and can actually suffer from problems before their time. Do not be afraid to be youthful, within reason. The next time you see a man in his seventies running a marathon or a woman keeping up in aerobic class, you can see that by refusing to give into age, they are healthier and live much longer lives.

218. _Regular Checkups_

It is crucial that you have regular checkups, which could include mammograms, pap smears, checks for colon cancer, EKGs, etc. Many times, a regular checkup could have caught something earlier on, actually saving a life. If you do not feel good, have your doctor check things out. If you are due for your annual mammogram, have it done. You could possibly be saving your own life.

219. _Cholesterol Levels_

High cholesterol leads to hardening of arteries, which in turn, leads to heart disease or attack. Keep your intake of food healthy, limit the amount of sugar you eat, and have your cholesterol checked. If it is higher than 200, ask your doctor for ways to reduce it.

220. _Meditate_

Find some time away from noise and distractions for you. Meditation can come in many forms. Whatever way you meditate, ensure that you are in a quiet place with soft lighting, sit with good posture and in a comfortable position, practice slow, rhythmic breathing, and concentrate on something calm and relaxing. Meditation is a great stress reducer, which is vital for good health.

221. _Listen to ME_

If you know that you are not feeling "right" but the doctor tells you everything is fine, listen to your body. There is nothing wrong with getting a second opinion. If you are not comfortable with the doctor's advice, get another exam. In addition, if you go to a doctor who tells you that what you feel is in your head, or you are crazy, get out of there immediately. You know your body better than anyone does and you need a doctor that believes in you and offers the right kind of support and encouragement.

222. _Body Fat_

When you think about losing weight, more importantly than weight is the amount of fat you are carrying around. This fat is measured with what is called Body Mass Index, or BMI. For women, if you are fit, your percent of body fat should range from 21% to 31%. If you are in incredible shape, that could be as low as 10%. For men, fit should be between 14% and 25%, and excellent shape, as low as 2%.

To calculate your body fat, write down how much you weigh (be honest – no one will see this but you). Multiply your weight by 703. Next, write down your height, in inches. Multiply by that same number. Then you will divide your weight number by your height number. That is your BMI. For example, if your weight were 150 pounds x 703, your weight answer would be 105,450. If your height is 5'4", that would be 64 inches x 64 for a total of 4,096. Taking the 105,450 divided by 4,096, you come out with a BMI of 25.7.

223. _Read the Label_

Get into a habit of reading the labels on food. While they may have messages such as "Low Fat" or "Reduced Calorie" written all over the front of the package or can, when you read the label and understand what you are looking for, you will probably be surprised. Regardless of what the claim may be, the label may tell another story. The FDA provides these important guidelines, therefore, should be what you look for. If the message and label do not jive, move on to a different product.

Fat-Free	Less than 0.5 grams of fat per serving, with no added fat or oil
Low fat	3 grams or less of fat per serving
Less fat	25% or less fat than the comparison food
Saturated Fat Free	Less than 0.5 grams of saturated fat and 0.5 grams of trans-fatty acids per serving

Cholesterol-Free	Less than 2 mg cholesterol per serving, and 2 grams or less saturated fat per serving
Low Cholesterol	20 mg or less cholesterol per serving and 2 grams or less saturated fat per serving
Reduced Calorie	At least 25% fewer calories per serving than the comparison food
Low Calorie	40 calories or less per serving
Extra Lean	Less than 5 grams of fat, 2 grams of saturated fat, and 95 mg of cholesterol per (100 gram) serving of meat, poultry or seafood
Lean	Less than 10 grams of fat, 4.5 g of saturated fat, and 95 mg of cholesterol per (100 gram) serving of meat, poultry or seafood
Light (fat)	50% or less of the fat than in the comparison food (ex: 50% less fat than our regular cheese)
Light (calories)	1/3 fewer calories than the comparison food
High-Fiber	5 grams or more fiber per serving
Sugar-Free	Less than 0.5 grams of sugar per serving
Sodium-Free or Salt-Free	Less than 5 mg of sodium per serving
Low Sodium	140 mg or less per serving
Very Low Sodium	35 mg or less per serving

224. *Water*

Water is excellent for the body and good health. Water helps flush out toxins and other unwanted things lingering in the body. Water also replenishes fluids that help lubricate the internal body, keeps you hydrated, reduces hunger, which helps with weight loss, and helps to make skin look smooth and young. If you are not used to drinking water, it may seem hard at first, but very quickly, you will enjoy the clean, refreshed way it makes you feel. At a minimum, you should drink 64-ounces a day and more if you can.

225. *Seatbelts*

You may be wondering what seatbelts have to do with health. Statistics show that wearing seatbelts keeps you safe and therefore allows you to live longer. To keep yourself safe and healthy, it is critical that you buckle up every time you get in *any* car. Do not be fooled into thinking that going the few blocks to the corner store is not big deal. Most accidents happen close to home so whether you are traveling one block or across the country, buckle up.

226. *Do Not Forget the Teeth*

Often the care of teeth and gums is overlooked as potential health risks. However, with the oral cavity being the main way in which parasites, bacteria, yeast, and fungus get into the body, taking time to thoroughly brush and floss your teeth is important. Keeping your mouth clean is a great way to benefit your health.

227. *Attitude*

A negative attitude can have a negative impact on your health just as a positive attitude can affect your health in a positive manner. Living well has a direct correlation with a positive outlook. Keep smiling and try to find the good in life, even when things are tough.

228. *Fighting Cancer*

With today's breakthroughs, there are many innovative ways to fight cancer. Although you may find this difficult to believe, the American Institute for Cancer Research has come up with a surprising way to fight cancer. After conducting thorough studies, researchers found that drinking tea, which contains antioxidants to help neutralize "free radicals" helps to fight cancer. While it is not a cure-all, if cancer runs in your family, it certainly will not hurt to add tea to your daily consumption.

229. _Be Careful with the Sun_

Everyone loves basking in the warm sun, especially if it is lying on a beautiful sandy beach. While the sun has many benefits, too much sun without proper protection can be harmful. Being sunburned not only hurts, but also damages skin and promotes wrinkles and cancer. If you are going to spend any time in the sun, even 10 minutes, protect your skin with sunscreen for both UVA and UVB rays.

230. _Tasty Almonds_

If you love nuts, then you are in luck. Almonds are not only delicious and make a great snack food, medical studies show they contain as much protein per ounce as red meat. In addition, they aid in reducing the risk of heart attacks by up to 50%. The next time you need something crunchy, reach for a handful of almonds.

231. _Wash your Hands_

This is something you have probably heard your whole life. Disease is easily spread from touch, whether from person to person or object to person. Giardia is the number one germ that is transferred from touching something infected. Once you have Giardia, you can get very ill. In addition, germs can be passed from your pet that has been rolling on the grass, something dropped on a dirty floor, just allow your imagine to roam if you dare. Washing your hands is a quick, easy way to reduce the spread of germs.

232. _Flaxseed_

A great way to maintain a healthy cardiovascular system is by adding flaxseed to your daily diet. Flaxseed actually contains what is called alpha-linolenic acid, which is a fatty acid essential in controlling blood pressure. They have a benefit of helping with digestion; just make sure the flaxseed is crushed for easier consumption and absorption.

233. *Give your Eyes a Rest*

Most jobs in today's society require the use of a computer. If you sit in front of a computer all day or work any job or hobby that requires your eyes to work hard, be sure to take breaks throughout your day. For soothing relief, you can use eye drops, close your eyes for a few minutes to allow them to rest, and look away to something other than what you are working on. Also, ensure that you are working with appropriate lighting, which is an oversight many people make. These are ways in which to give your eyes a much-needed break. Eyestrain can cause eye problems as well as headaches.

234. *Watch the Sugar*

Often people think by drinking fruit juices or eating low-fat fruit roll-ups and such, they are cutting out or eliminating sugar. The fact is that some fruit juices have more sugar than a soda. Reduction of sugar is important to good health; therefore always check out the sugar content of anything you put in your mouth, even if it appears to be healthy.

235. *Throw out the Scales*

If you have bathroom scales, you should either get rid of them or put them away for a while. Weight does not accurately reflect the level of your fitness. If you should be measuring anything, it should be body fat, not the weight.

236. *Sunscreen*

Most people know that sunscreen is important for shoulders, backs, legs, and arms when out in the sun but there are other parts of the body that are often overlooked. When enjoying the beautiful sun, be sure to use sunscreen on your ears, slips, and even the tops of your feet as well!

237. _Aspirin versus Ibuprofen_

Both of these products can help in certain situations. For example, aspirin is an analgesic, used for pain while ibuprofen is both an analgesic and anti-inflammatory. Therefore, the next time you have to deal with sore muscles after a good workout, remember that you can get some needed relief from these over the counter remedies.

238. _Berries, Berries, Berries_

Ah, the sweet taste of fresh berries! Berries are actually good for you and contain plant nutrients called anthocyanidins. These are incredible antioxidants and some have high levels of resveratrol, which helps fight heart disease and cancer. The next time you want something sweet, juicy, and good for you, reach for blueberries, grapes, or strawberries, and do not feel guilty!

239. _Some like it Hot_

Hot, spicy foods that contain curry, chilies, or other hot peppers such as cayenne, help to trigger endorphins. These hormones are what make people feel good and well balanced. In fact, endorphins are like a natural morphine that helps ease pain and provide a sense of well being. The next time you are feeling a little down or have some minor pain, try eating something spicy.

240. _Beware of Allergies/Reactions_

Pay attention to what you eat. With so many wonderful restaurants, trying new dishes is exciting and fun. However, several foods are responsible for up to 90% of all allergy problems. If you notice after eating certain foods you suffer from headaches, upset stomach, or other problems, make note, you could be having an allergic reaction. The foods most likely the problem include eggs, milk, peanuts, tree nuts, soy, shellfish, and fish. For children, the common foods include cow's milk, soy, eggs, and wheat.

241. _Breast Exams_

Make sure you conduct regular breast examines. This can quickly and painlessly be done during your shower or lying down when going to bed. Contact your primary physician or gynecologist for a free pamphlet showing the proper way this is done. Taking proactive steps could save your life.

242. _Asthmatics and Sports_

If you suffer from asthma, you already know that some sports should be avoided, depending on the severity. If you have trouble on a daily basis and love sports, be encouraged to know that some sports are asthma-friendly and in fact, can be helpful in that they help make the lungs stronger. These sports include swimming, cycling, and fishing, walking, and canoeing. Again, check with your physician before getting involved with any sport if you have a health condition.

243. _Fragrance and Aging_

If you want to do everything you can to age gracefully, you should avoid anything that has the perfumes or lotions of coconut oil and orange. The reason is that these fragrances contain a substance called psoralen, which is known to speed up the aging process.

244. _Circulation and Lymph Glands_

When you finish with your bath or shower, you can actually help your body's circulation and improvement in which lymph glands drain, all by the way that you towel off your body. Very simply, when drying your arms and legs as well as torso, always towel away toward the groin for your legs and toward your armpits for the arms and torso. This might sound funny, but studies have shown this works.

245. _Make Time for Intimacy_

If you are married, be sure to make time for intimacy in your relationship. Sex is a great stress reducer and keeps a marriage happy. Sex is healthy act that should be enjoyed.

246. _No More Caffeine_

Caffeine can dehydrate your body so try to remove it from your daily intake. This may require some weaning, but when done, you will feel better. If you feel that you need something, instead of grabbing a cub of caffeinated coffee or soda, try drinking herbal tea.

247. _Stick with Whole Wheat_

Whole wheat is actually better for you. It offers more fiber, which helps reduce the risk of heart disease, stroke, cancer, diverticulosis, diabetes to name a few. When possible, set aside the white flour and bread and reach for products that are made from oats, barley, buckwheat, bulgur, rye, brown rice, millet, and wheat.

248. _What are Flavonoids?_

These are oestrogen-like compounds found in plants that act as hormone blockers any place in the body where there are excess hormones that could cause such cancers such as breast cancer. Flavonoids are also strong antioxidants, which can be found in foods such as beans, onions, broccoli, apples, and soy products.

249. _Green Tea_

Studies have shown that adding green tea to your daily diet provides several health benefits to include the metabolizing of fat, ease of digestion, and is a good source of flavonoids. Another benefit is that tea is a form of natural diuretic, which is very mild and not harmful.

250. *Sodium*

As a way of reducing blood pressure, which is bad on the heart, reduce the amount of sodium (salt) you intake. You may be thinking of table salt but you should know that many canned vegetables, soups, even soda, are very high in sodium. Look at your labels and try to cut back on processed foods. If you have a craving for salt, switch to natural seasoning and just a little salt.

251. *Family History*

If you are not sure what your family history is in relation to health, now is a good time to find out. This can be especially true if you are adopted or disconnected from immediately family members. There might be certain types of cancer, diabetes, asthma, or other illnesses that you could get a jump on if you knew they were prevalent in your family. Once you discover any risks, talk with your physician for recommendations.

252. *Puffy Eyes*

If you battle with puffy eyes or dark circles that make you look worn out, do not feel alone. This is actually a very common complaint that can be treated easily. By using a mixture of Vitamin C ester and alpha-lipoic acid eye therapy, you will find that this antibiotic helps reduce this puffiness.

253. *Control those Cravings*

If you are like any other person on the face of the planet, you have cravings for sweet foods. To help with these cravings, you can use Normoglycaemia to help normalize your blood glucose levels. This supplement is very rich in magnesium, B Vitamins, and Chromium and has been proven successful for many years.

FITNESS

Fitness is just as important as health, and in reality, fitness correlates directly with our health. If we are not taking care of our bodies, we get sick. Here are some great recommendations to keep fit:

254. *Bicycling*

When you ask many adults when the last time they rode a bike is, they cannot answer. Although bicycling is a favorite pastime, many adults do not take advantage of this great option for exercise. Not only does bike riding exercise the body and build a stronger cardiovascular system, it allows you to get out and enjoy nature, fresh air, and see new sites.

255. *Jogging or Walking*

Both jogging and walking are GREAT ways to get fit. Not only do they tone the muscles, relieve stress, create a healthier heart, and improve lung capability, they make you look wonderful, which in turns helps you get excited about doing other exercise for fitness.

256. *Swimming*

Swimming is an excellent way to get into and stay in shape. If you do not own a pool, many high schools have aquatic centers, or there is always the YWCA or YMCA, or your local gym. Many offer water aerobic classes that will help you tighten your body, lose weight, and get a good overall workout.

257. *Tennis Anyone*

Tennis is not only a fun sport, but also a great way to exercise. You do not have to be a Venice Williams to play; in fact, you do not even have to be good. Just running after the ball alone will help get you into shape. This is a great way to strengthen your cardiovascular system and lose weight. You can find tennis courts in just about every city and if you would like to play but have no idea how, lessons are reasonable.

258. _Dancing_

Dancing is so much fun and whether you enjoy a slow, Ballroom dance or a nightclub packed with people all moving to heart-pumping techno, as long as you are moving, it really does not matter what type of dance or music. The whole idea is to move your body. Dancing has long been recommended as an avenue to fitness.

259. _VCR_

If you have a VCR or DVD, rather than just using it for your favorite comedy or action-packed movie, try sticking in some good workout tapes. Even taking 15 minutes every day to workout will get you started. Try that for two weeks and you will be surprised at the results. Once you see that 15 minutes a day makes a difference, you will be encouraged to increase the time spent.

260. _Abdominal Crunches_

While you may not end up with a washboard stomach, you can do some things to get your abdomen in better shape. Crunches have long been a favorite for many athletes for the very reason that they work. Lying on your back with knees bent, keeping feet flat on the floor, cross your hands across your chest and then curl your torso, rolling from your sternum toward your hips. Do this slowly and start out with a set of ten crunches in three reps. In other words, do ten crunches, wait a minute, do ten more, wait a minute, and then do the final ten. As you get accustomed to these, you can increase both the number of sets and reps.

261. _Squats_

Squats are excellent for glutes, hamstrings, quads, and calves. With your feet standing firm and spread apart about two feet, bend your knees slightly. Then, very smoothly, you will squat toward the floor without going all the way down. This usually takes some practice but within a short period, you will enjoy the benefits.

262. *Tricep Press*

Having firm arms is something that many people focus on when exercising. For an Overhead Tricep Press, standing on the floor with your feet about two feet apart, knees slightly bent, you will extend your arms over your head. Keep your elbows locked and then very slowly lower your hands behind your head. You want to do this with some type of weight, but small weights like one to five pounds. If you do not have weights of your own, you can hold a one-pound of vegetables, which will work perfectly.

263. *Get to the Gym*

Working out at home is a good option and for some people, they are committed enough to actually make it work. However, for the majority of people wanting to get into shape, the inspiration, competitiveness, and encouragement received from working out in a gym is the way to go. Although it will require a small investment, make the decision to find a gym that offers state-of-the-art equipment, qualified staff, and fun classes where you can enjoy working out.

264. *Eat More*

Before you get too excited, understand that when you eat, it is not how much you eat, but what you eat. If you find that getting fit and eating less food is too hard, add more of the right food into your diet. Great options include an orange, hard-boiled egg, small broiled chicken breast, and fresh vegetables such as carrots, celery sticks. If you have a craving for something sweet, many delicious options are available such as Weight Watchers cheesecake or Chocolate Éclairs. Getting fit does not mean total deprivation.

265. *Network at the Gym*

Getting to the gym is a great way to get fit. However, there are other benefits to going to the gym. You will have the opportunity to expand your social ring by making new friends, all working to get fit just like you. This will provide needed encouragement, which in turn helps you to stay motivated.

266. *Tight Muscles*

In addition to a good aerobic exercise, you should add weight training in, which will help balance out the fitness routine and provide you with the best results. If you are not sure where to start, a professional trainer can help get you started on a healthy program.

267. *Heat Therapy*

Using heat therapy is a great way to reduce long-term effects or injury for overworked muscles. If you have sore muscles and joints, use heat to help increase blood flow, relieve muscle spasms, and increase joint mobility.

268. *Before it's a Problem*

Instead of taking an injury through rehabilitation after it is an injury, why not rehab before. You can actually take preventative measures before you indulge in a sport or activity by ensuring you stretch properly. This will help strengthen as well as stretch muscles, which in turn, helps reduce unnecessary injuries.

269. *Running in the Sand*

If you live in a geographical area, where you have the luxury of sandy beaches, and if you are in the process of rehabilitating your knees, ankles, and even some injuries to the back, you should avoid running in the sand during this time. The reason is that running on sand actually produces greater force on the joints.

270. *Quick Energy*

Listen to your body. If you find that you are dragging, eat the right foods that will give your body the energy needed and are healthy. Examples of these foods include carrots, rice cakes, breakfast cereals, bananas, and potatoes.

271. *Quality Matters*

While finding that great bargain on poorly made running or training shoes may be tempting, it would be far better to put your workout on hold for a couple of weeks while you save the money needed to purchase a good pair. That does not mean you have to pay a fortune, but always ensure you are working out with the proper shoes. Wearing shoes that have a poor design or poor durability can actually cause injury.

272. *Get Ready to Run*

Before any workout, always warm up. If you are a runner, before you go out for your actual run, take two to five minutes to jog in place to prepare. You will find that you have a better run.

273. *Increased Protein*

Many diets of today's society pull you back and forth, one telling you to eat more protein, and one less. The fact is that if you are not exercising as much as you used to or if you are exercising heavily, your body could in fact need more protein than what the RDA recommends. The good balance for either scenario is 50% to 60% carbohydrates, 20% to 25% protein and 20% or less of fat. If you stick with this equation, you will benefit.

274. *Asthma and Exercise*

If you have asthma and love to exercise, it is important to keep your inhaler with you. However, if for some reason you forget, remember that caffeine can provide temporary relieve of bronchia constriction. If you do not have asthma but after years of running, you develop breathing problems, you could be suffering from "Exercise Induced Asthma", which should be mentioned to your physician.

275. _Resistance_

The next time you work out try adding some resistance to your routine. You can use special rubber bands or other devices designed specifically as a way to help you with isometrics, thus get better results.

276. _Taking a Break_

If you are actively involved in a workout regimen but you are getting ready to go on vacation for two weeks or have an extra heavy workload for your job over the next couple of weeks, instead of just stopping your routine completely during that time, just cut back. Even reducing your workout by 50% will give you the break you need but also make it much easier to get back to full speed than if you just stopped altogether.

277. _Exercise and Summer_

Exercising outdoors can be refreshing and fun but it can also cause problems if you do not follow some simple rules. Make sure you are drinking enough water, about 16 ounces every 30 minutes, before, during, and after exercise. Some sports drinks such as PowerAid and GatorAid have special ingredients that help replenish fluids to prevent dehydration.

278. _Be Realistic_

It would be great to be able to jump right into a hard workout, feel great, and see instant results. However, it is important to be realistic about several things. First, you need to understand that you more than likely will not (or should not) start out with a hard workout if you have not been in a regular exercise routine. Start out slow and do not set yourself up for failure by expecting miracles overnight. Getting fit takes time and with commitment, you will reach your goals.

279. *Envision Success*

Try to envision how great you will look and feel once you get in shape. If you can, find a picture of someone that has the same body type and pin it up where you can look at it every day to help you see the same results you too can reach with hard work and time.

280. *Pregnancy and Exercise*

Do not think that just because you are pregnant means you have to stop exercising, unless you have special needs. Before you exercise during pregnancy, always check with your doctor first. Once you get permission to proceed, you will find that leg extensions, standing curls, and other exercises can be done with ease. If you are not sure what you can and cannot do, ask your doctor for recommendations.

281. *Track Progress*

Often when trying to get in shape, it seems like you are working hard and sweating, but getting nowhere. In actuality, things are happening, just not yet seen. Keep track of two things in particular. First, track your measurements. You will probably be surprised within only a few weeks at the progress made. Second, track your routines so you can determine what is working for you and what is not as successful.

282. *Medication and Exercise*

If you are on scheduled prescription medication, you should know that some drugs could have a negative affect if mixed with exercise. Some can cause the heart to work too hard or you might not sweat as needed, to mention a few. If you are taking medication, before you start any exercise program, consult with your physician to ensure there are no harmful effects.

283. _Cool Down_

Just as warming up for exercise is important, cooling down after exercise is just as important. Once you have completed your workout, take five to 10 minutes to walk, or stretch to allow your body to cool down. This is very important for the muscles and joints and for the heart and lung.

284. _Walk the Dog_

Instead of just opening the back door to let the dogs out, put them on a leash and go for a nice walk. They will appreciate the new scenery and you are doing yourself a great justice.

285. _Lunchtime_

Instead of eating a heavy lunch, put together something light and easy and go for a walk. You can sip on a protein drink or snack on fruit while enjoying a nice brisk walk before heading back to the office. You will feel refreshed and more invigorated for your afternoon tasks.

286. _Bowling_

Get some exercise by joining a bowling league. You can find a league for just about every level of bowler as well as any day and time of the week. This is a great way to get out and have some fun while also exercising. Yes, bowling does count as exercising.

287. _Set Goals_

Set a goal for yourself, perhaps four to six weeks. By breaking up your time into workable chunks of time instead of looking out an entire year, you will have a much easier time meeting your goals and staying on track as well as encouraged.

288. _Neurobics_

This is a new term coined by researchers from the United States relating to ways in which to get the brain activated with its own biochemical pathways. The goal is to have the brain strengthened and energetic. Positive thinking has long been proven to help with illness and disease so the theory is that an energetic mind is also good for fitness.

289. _Fitness and Food_

Certain foods provide specific benefits for people who workout. If you need quick energy or planning to run a 4K or 10K and need to accelerate your metabolism, bread, grain-based food, sugar, and honey are great choices. If your goal is to burn fat, you should eat peas, oat bran, pasta, rice, beans, lentils, and soya beans.

290. _Interval Training_

As a way to improve your fitness in a speedy manner and lose weight, try interval training. This means that you where your workout intensity varies. This is beneficial to your workout and fights workout boredom.

291. _After Exercise_

When you have completed your exercise regimen, instead of eating carbohydrates, grab some fresh fruit or water. The reason is that for a minimum of an hour after exercise, the body is still breaking down fat. You need to allow the body to finish doing its job.

292. _Breath in – Breath out_

You might wonder what breathing has to do with fitness and the truth is it has a lot to do with it. When exercising, there is a proper way to breath that will help you with the appropriate amount of oxygen into the system but will also help you with endurance. For example, marathon runners will tell you that they use a rhythm when running that allows them to runner longer and healthier than normal breathing.

293. *Circle of Friends*

When trying to get into shape, it is important to have family and friends in support. This means they need to respect your goals and not offer you wrong foods, or try to pull you away from your exercise program. Explain to them how important this is to you and that you need their encouragement.

294. *Know your Age*

While you are only as old as you feel, keep in mind that young people can very easily leap over an obstacle in the garage or take a nice jog through the neighborhood with no problem. However, as people age, it is crucial to stay fit and healthy and pay attention to your age. Something that might have been easy for you when you were young may now cause injury or illness. If you find you can no longer perform one activity, do not be discouraged; just substitute one activity for another.

295. *Diabetes and Exercise*

Aerobic exercise can actually be beneficial for people with diabetes. This exercise increases the insulin sensitivity and when combined with good eating, can help restore a normal glucose metabolism. Before starting into a workout program, you need to see your doctor first to determine if there are any risks for coronary artery disease and that your blood glucose control is appropriate for exercise. Once cleared, you will feel better and see for you the benefits associated with exercise.

296. *Golf Injuries*

While golf is not a high impact sport, injuries can still occur. One such injury associated with golf is torn rotator cuffs. To avoid this from happening to you, it is important to keep your muscles strengthened and flexible. Simple stretching can help tremendously. When you stretch, take it slow, only going to a point of mild tension. Each stretch should be held for 20 to 40 seconds with smooth motion (no bouncing). Just as it is important to stretch before you golf, it is equally as important to stretch after golf.

297. *Stretch the Mind*

When you stretch your body in preparation for exercise as well as after exercise, you need to stretch your mind as well. You might be wondering how and why. When your mind is relaxed, your body follows. To achieve a relaxed mind, listen to soothing music, relax your breathing, and use visualization techniques such as Yoga. Another exercise discipline that are very popular and works is the Pilates program.

298. *Proper Equipment*

Okay, the scenario is that you have made your New Year's resolution and are determined to get into shape. Too embarrassed to head to the gym just yet, you make the decision to purchase some equipment such as a Nordic Trac or treadmill to get in better shape before being seen in public. While that is a common occurrence, it is important to make sure you buy the right equipment and equipment in good working order. Many people will sell equipment at a huge discount in the local paper, making the buy look too good to pass up. However, while most are honest sales, some are selling the equipment because it does not work or something is wrong with it. This could lead to further injury so when buying from a private party, bring someone with you who knows about workout equipment or contact the maker of that particular piece of equipment and ask them what to look for to ensure you are buying a good piece of equipment.

299. *Beauty is Skin Deep*

Accept the fact that everyone's body is built different and when God created you, He did not make a mistake. When you see the models and Hollywood stars on the cover of those glamour magazines, keep in mind that every one of those photographs have been airbrushed, meaning they really do not look like that. While they make look fantastic either way, you are not those people - you are you! Always love yourself for who you are inside. As long as you are eating right, exercising, and doing the best for yourself, then you should be happy. You may never reach that model appearance and to be honest, you do not want to. Do the best you can and love the inside beauty more than the outside beauty!

300. *Built-in Air-Conditioner*

Your body was created with a built in cooling system, called sweat or if you prefer, perspiration. On television and in magazines, you will find numerous advertisements encouraging deodorant for exercise when in actuality; sweat is a vital key in a good workout. When your body heats up do to exertion, sweat is doing the job intended – keeping the body cool. Therefore, do not try to squelch sweating, accept it.

301. *Heat Exhaustion and Heat Stroke*

Heat-related illnesses can be a common occurrence when exerting energy in the outdoors or poorly ventilated indoors. Two primary contributors can be alcohol consumption and not enough water. Three types of illness include heat cramps, which are very painful and might be combined with headache or nausea, heat exhaustion, which is more serious and includes vomiting, chills, headache, dizziness, among other symptoms, and heatstroke, which if the most dangerous and if not caught and treated immediately, can be fatal or lead to permanent brain damage or coma. For all three of these, particularly the last two, the best action is prevention. If you notice that your heart starts beating too fast and you feel light-headed, get out of the sun. Wear loose fitting clothing, preferably made from lightweight cotton as well as light colors. Drink LOTS of water. Even if you do not feel thirsty, drink anyway. Do not go with the old rule of taking salt tablets. You should always stay clear of these unless you have first consulted with your physician. Stay away from alcohol, soft drinks, caffeine, or heavily sugared drinks to include fruit juice. Take frequent breaks and if necessary, stop for the day. If you do believe you are in trouble, seek medical attention immediately. It is far better safe than sorry!

302. *Check your Pulse*

As you exercise, it is to your advantage to keep track of your pulse rate. You can pick up an inexpensive pulse measure at any local Wal-mart, K-Mart, or sporting good store. This will measure your heart rate to ensure you are staying within a healthy range. The rate is measured by counting the beats of your heart in a set amount of time, usually about 15 to 20 seconds, and then multiplying the number of beats to get your number of beats per minute. For example, if your pulse at 20 seconds were 40, since there are 60 seconds in a minute, you would take 40 times three for a total rate per minute of 120.

303. *Safety First*

Whatever you do, if you are involved in a sport or activity that has potential for injury, specifically head injury, use the proper equipment no matter what anyone else tells you. For example, if you are involved with skateboarding and this is how you stay in shape, good for you! However, you need to wear protective gear such as a helmet, gloves, knee guards, etc. Most people think that something significant has to happen in order to get a head in jury. Unfortunately, that is a huge misconception. The truth is that falling one foot onto the pavement and hitting your head is enough to cause serious injury or death. This is the time to put your pride aside and think of safety first.

By taking care of your body through good health habits and fitness, you will live a happier, better, and longer life!

Part 4 - 101 Ways to Build Happy, Lasting Relationships

Dating and marriage is different than it was twenty years ago. In today's society, more than 50% of all marriages fail for one reason or another. Just thinking about that makes "commitment" seem scary. It seems that when relationships are faced with challenges, people quit trying. Dating is more like a marathon, trying to date as many people as possible, instead of taking time to get to know someone at a deeper level. For married couples, divorce is not biased. Whether married for thirty years or eight months, the outcome can be the same.

The fact is that relationships, whether dating or married, are hard. Things do not always go perfectly, fighting does occur, and it takes a 100% commitment from both parties to make it a success. Often when people break off a relationship, they feel as though something is missing. The "spark" has gone, leaving one or both people feeling inadequate and unfulfilled.

However, even though the odds are not very good, healthy, and long-lasting relationships are definitely possible and proven by many people. Look at Paul Newman and Joanne Woodard, Danny Devito and Rhea Perlman, or Nancy and Ronald Regan. What secrets do they possess? The answer is that they all work hard at their relationship. They made a decision of choosing to love their mate rather than relying on the "warm and fuzzy" feelings, which everyone knows will fade. By making love a choice you are making a decision that even in the bad times, you stick it out.

Think of it like choosing a car. You pick out the make, model, year, color, and features that you believe are best for you. After driving your car for a couple of months, you realize that perhaps you should have purchased a larger car, or that maybe the leather seats would have been better, or on hot sunny days, the sunroof would have been nice. However, it is now too late so you choose to keep your car and make it work. It is the same for marriage. Not everything will be perfect and there will be major obstacles to overcome but you have made your decision and now you choose to make it work.

There are hundreds of things you can do to better your relationship. To help get you headed in the right direction, we have chosen 101 ways to build, strengthen, and enhance your relationship.

Remember, little steps taken every day will add up to big successes.

304. *Start Over*

When couples first get together, everything is new and exciting. They overlook the little annoying things the other person does. However, after time, the nagging starts, instead of hearing, "You look beautiful," they might hear "Why are you wearing that shirt?" If this sounds like your relationship, first, the two of you need to sit down and be honest that things have changed. Identify the things each other did in the beginning of the relationship that created the attraction in the first place. Then together, make a commitment to start over. The truth is, both of you will have to work on this. It will not automatically be easy but it is possible. Start by forgiving each other, forgetting the past, and then start over with the flirtation. Focus only on the special things your mate does and relearn to put the unimportant things aside. It will take some time so be patient.

305. *Schedule Time*

Spending quality time together is crucial. This time can be with friends, dining out, attending a sporting event, or cuddling together while watching a favorite movie. The activity is not what is important but the fact that you are together, doing something that you both enjoy. People have extremely busy schedules and between work, family, the home, errands, and everything else going on, finding time for your mate can be difficult. Just as you would schedule a meeting on your calendar, show some courtesy in the relationship by scheduling time with each other. Once the plan is in place, no backing out unless you have some life and death emergency.

306. *The Power of Touch*

When a child is ill, doctors will tell you that it is proven that a simple, loving touch of a parent can quickly pull the child through a crisis. It is the same for relationships. Playing with your mate's hair, rubbing their hand, a soft kiss on the neck, a soft pat on the leg or giving a gentle back rub will make a huge difference in how your mate responds to you. When was the last time you walked up to your mate for no reason and without saying a word, affectionately placed a kiss on their neck? This is not in a sexual way, but an affectionate way. There is a difference. The next time the two of you are sitting in the car, at the grocery story, or standing in line at the theater, quietly reach over and take their hand. Do not be surprised if you get a strange look of curiosity the first time!

307. *Surprise*

If you and your mate have scheduled some time for a Friday night dinner, put together a surprise instead. For example, if your mate loves professional wrestling, buy some tickets near the front or if they like concerts, purchase the tickets ahead of time, getting the best seats possible. When Friday night comes around, insist on driving and head toward the location where the event is taking place. When asked where you are going, simply answer, "I have a surprise for you. I know you love professional wrestling so I purchased two great seats for tonight's performance," or "I know we had planned on going to dinner, but I wanted to surprise you with something special. I purchased tickets to see one of your favorite groups in concert." The idea of you getting the tickets for something THEY like and then keeping it as a special surprise will touch the heart!

308. *Needed Space*

As important as it is to spend quality time together, it is equally important to give each other time to do something they like. If your mate loves to fish but you have no desire to bait a hook with little, slimy worms, or if you like to go to the casino but your mate would rather do something different, encourage each other to take time apart. Try establishing a set time for this very purpose, if possible. For example, perhaps you could determine that every other Friday night is "singles" night. This is not a time to date other people, but to enjoy preferred activities. Remember that you have to place trust in your relationship. If you try this and then drill them, to see what they did, whom they were with, and where they went, then the exercise has failed.

309. _No Debates_

If you know that you and your mate have proven differences in opinion on certain subjects, avoid those subjects. As an example, if you are a Republican and your mate is a Democrat, politics should probably be avoided. As the two of you identify new topics that could cause a debate session, stop the conversation before it even gets started.

310. _Filler Talk_

If you are married, especially with children, break out of the habit of talking about nothing. Many times, families will be sitting around the dinner table and the conversation consists of, "Do you like your carrots?", or "I wonder what is on TV tonight?" Instead, change your strategy to include real questions, showing real interest. Replace the normal, "Did you have a good day at work?" with "Tell me what you did at work today." Even if you do not understand everything being said, listen with interest. It is not that you are so much interested in the work, but your mate's life.

311. _Re-establish Old Traditions_

If you and your mate had a tradition of some kind when you first got together, dust it off and breathe life back into it. Perhaps you met after work on Friday at the local pub for a drink, washed your cars together every Saturday morning, or attended church together on Sunday. Whatever it was, re-establish the tradition.

312. *Predictability*

If asking couples the factors involved in the demise of their relationship, one of the common responses is that everything in the relationship is so predictable. When rebuilding a relationship, do not be afraid of letting go of boredom. If you normally hate the fact that Saturday afternoons consist of your mate sitting for hours watching football, fix some finger sandwiches and something cool to drink and go join them on the couch, or if your mate spends hours in the garden trying to make things look perfect, surprise them with a new flowering plant, and then help to plant it. When taking a walk with your mate, stop and give them a soft kiss, say, "I love you," and then keep walking. Take some chances and do the unexpected.

313. *Lighten Up*

Often when couples have gone through or are going through some bumpy spots in their relationship, things tend to get serious. It could be that there is a tremendous amount of tension or perhaps they are not sure what to say. Regardless of the reason, learn to lighten up. Do not take every comment, glance, or movement as a serious problem. If your mate makes a mistake, which you both will, let it go, or if appropriate, laugh about it. If you make a mistake, do not be afraid to poke fun at yourself. This will automatically start the process of tension breaking.

314. *Communicate*

When couples are having problems in a relationship, communication is the first thing to stop. It is often easier to just be quiet than to get mad. When rebuilding relationships, just as communication was the first to stop, it now needs to be the first to start. This will require that both individuals let down their guard and pretty much throw caution to the wind. Healing in the relationship cannot start until you talk. Make an agreement that you will talk about anything and everything and that you will listen, really listen. That does not mean that you will agree with everything, which is perfectly fine. However, if you do not agree, do not yell, rather, the two of you need to calmly discuss the issue and together, work out a solution. This is hard work but within a very short time, you will both feel much better, individually and as a couple.

315. *A Night of Passion*

Intimacy and passion in relationships is not only important but also healthy. Couples need to enjoy being together in an intimate way. When relationships are troubled, the last thing either person wants is to be sexual or passionate with each other. However, this is a part of the healing and rebuilding of the relationship and although it might be awkward in the beginning, it is crucial. Make your intimate time together special. Surprise your mate with a warm bubble bath, lighted candles, soft music, and a bottle of wine, or reserve a nice romantic evening at a local hotel to include a wonderful candlelit dinner, fine wine, and a beautiful room.

316. *Dinner Party*

Start a new tradition of hosting a dinner party every other month or two and inviting several of you and your mate's friends. Set up board games that everyone will enjoy, have some light and lively music playing, and plan to have a blast. Spending time with friends in this kind of setting is a great way to reduce stress. When stress is low, couples get along better. This is a wonderful way to interact with each other's friends as a couple.

317. *Happy Birthday*

As people grow older, in general, birthdays become less celebrated. Gifts are quickly given, meals eaten, and it is over. For your mate's next birthday, take some time to plan something very special. Make this a true celebration of their life as a way of showing your love and appreciation. Every person, even adults, like attention and love to be appreciated. Whether a surprise party or not, your mate will be impressed that you went to all the effort just for them.

318. *Secret Getaway*

Plan a nice weekend getaway to some place off the beaten track where you can enjoy some privacy. A quaint cottage or charming bed and breakfast would be ideal choices. Scout out the area ahead of time and choose a few things that the two of you would like to do in the area but just be sure to leave plenty of time for you to enjoy some alone time. Order a nice bottle of wine or some hot cappuccino and relax in front of the fire! Make this a romantic weekend where you can rekindle your love.

319. *Special Greeting*

If your mate has to work late and you know he had a bad day, surprise him with a late-night gourmet meal. When you hear him arrive home, greet him in new, sexy lingerie, a warm kiss, and wonderful hot meal. After he picks himself up off the floor, he will fall in love with you all over again for this wonderful greeting.   If reversed and the woman is coming home, after giving her a lingering kiss, have her join you in the dining room where the table is set with soft glowing candles and a wonderful meal. Have an envelope lying by her plate that when opened, she will read, "This certificate is good for one thirty-minute massage after dinner." This is how you keep romance alive!

320. *Just Because*

Give your mate gifts "just because." These do not have to be expensive whatsoever. For example, one woman had a miniature dish collection in her kitchen. Her husband came home and told her that he had a gift for her. Holding out her hand, he gently placed in her hand a miniature porcelain cup with her name neatly written in blue ink. She knew that this cup probably cost no more than $2.00 but the thought that he would take the time to find something she enjoyed, was worth $1 million. The small gifts packed with thought are far more cherished.

321. *Say it with Words*

Surprise your mate with little notes found in unexpected places. If your mate travels for work, place a loving note somewhere in their suitcase. Perhaps they have a long commute to work. If so, slip a note saying, "I love you," in their CD case where you know they will find it. Another recommendation is sticking a note on the bathroom mirror so this will be the first thing seen in the morning. Be creative and have some fun with this.

322. *Cuddle Time*

When couples first start dating, cuddling is usually a part of their everyday existence. However, as the relationship progresses or after children enter the picture, the cuddling stops. Take some time just to cuddle. If your mate is sitting on the couch watching a movie, or laying in bed reading, scoot close and tell them that you just want to cuddle. This makes both people feel secure and loved.

323. *Breakfast in Bed*

When was the last time you or your mate were served breakfast in bed? Never? On a Saturday or Sunday, when nothing special is planned, get up a little early and fix their favorite breakfast. Include the morning newspaper as an added bonus. Although they may be shocked, you can be guaranteed that this gesture of love will be appreciated.

324. *Make the Men Feel Good*

For the man in your life, here are some recommendations for making him feel special:

- Flirt with him in public places
- Just once, leave the toilet lid *up*
- Lavish him with compliments
- Tell him how sexy he is
- Act jealous once in awhile, even if you are not
- Remind him that he is a wonderful mate, husband, father, whichever applies
- Tell him how handsome you find him

325. *Make the Women Feel Good*

Just like men, woman love feeling good about themselves. These recommendations might help:

- Tell her how beautiful she is
- Compliment her on her many skills (be specific)
- Just once, leave the toilet seat *down*
- Tell her how much she means to you
- Let her know that she is your best friend
- Show affectionate to her in front of family and friends
- Let her know that you find her to be sexy

326. *That Kiss*

As couples become comfortable with each other, kisses can become lame. Get rid of the pecks and get serious with the kisses. The next time the two of you greet each other, enjoy your kiss and do not be so quick to stop. While there are appropriate times for serious kissing, they should be loving, sincere, and passionate, regardless of how long they last. You will find that as you pay attention to your kissing and let your mate know that you enjoy kissing them, you will both feel better about your relationship.

327. *Be Kind to One Another*

Unbelievably, kindness is often over simplified. Even good relationships can lack acts of kindness. This refers to "Do unto others…" Simple acts of kindness can have huge impacts on a relationship. If your husband or boyfriend is out working on the car on a hot summer day, make a thermos of ice-cold tea and take it to him, giving him a gentle kiss. If your wife or girlfriend has been working at the computer all day, walk up behind her and massage her shoulders and neck. You get the idea. Kindness means looking at the other person's situation and seeing what you can do or add to that situation to make it better or easier. This is a way to validate your respect for each other. Kindness will go a long way in a relationship.

Find some type of hobby that you both enjoy and then do it together. It might be that you both love refurnishing furniture. Turn this into an adventure of going to estate sales together to find nice pieces of furniture and them refurbishing them as a team. Another option would be if you have both wanted to learn how to ballroom or salsa dance. Take lessons together so you can then go out on the town and dance the night away. This is a great way to make your relationship even stronger while adding in something fun that you both enjoy.

329. *Listen – Really Listen*

Get into a habit of listening to what your mate is saying. Not the kind of listening that you do when you go out or sit at the dinner table, but a different kind of listening. Have you ever overheard your mate make a comment to a friend or family member about something they really want or want to do? Maybe you heard your boyfriend or husband tell a friend that they would love a certain tool. For no reason whatsoever, make a special effort to get that for him. You might have heard your girlfriend or wife mention a spa that they would love to try. Again, without any reason, surprise her. This shows that your mate is really paying attention to things important to you.

330. *Be a Kid*

Do not be a prude. There is absolutely no reason why couples at any age cannot get into tickling matches or wrestle on the floor. Do not allow your relationship to grow old and stale. Understand and accept that it is perfectly fine to be silly from time to time. If you have nothing special planned on a Friday night, rent a few games, order in Chinese, plug in the Play Station, and play games.

331. *All Decked Out*

Although most people do not get dressed formally to go out, as a special treat, find an upscale restaurant, the opera, or even a ball, where the man can wear a tuxedo and the woman an evening gown. If possible, rent a limousine and have a bottle of champagne chilling before you get in. You will both feel good about yourselves and spending this magical evening together. This is something unique that brings another unexpected twist into the relationship, which keeps things interesting and alive. The two of you will have a romantic night that you will never forget.

332. *Showing Love*

Although hearing the words, "I love you" is special and important, sometimes you wish you could tell your mate as well as hear from your mate those words, but in special and unique ways. Here are some ideas of how this can be accomplished:

- Rent his favorite movie, even if it is something you do not like, and plan an evening alone where you can be with him as he enjoys his special treat.
- When he gets out of the shower, hand him a warm, cozy towel just heated in the dryer.
- When you make him pancakes, first pour the words, "I Love You" on the griddle and cook for a minute to brown. Then, pour more batter over the words to create a round pancake. The result will be a pancake displaying those three special words when you flip it over.
- While he is out of town, wash his car and surprise him by picking him up in a clean, shiny car at the airport.
- Take him out to lunch.
- Have his favorite breakfast on the table along with the morning newspaper.
- Instead of bugging him to go to the grocery store with you, let him stay home.
- Display your favorite picture of the two of you on the refrigerator.
- Buy him a subscription to his favorite magazine.

333. *Split the Responsibility*

Whether dating or married, weekends are always full of errands and chores. If you find that on the weekend things are lopsided, help your mate out. For example, if there are kids involved and one has a soccer game while the other has a baseball game, at the same time, offer to take one of the kids and your mate take the other. Make this a special time by packing a special lunch or snacks. Perhaps one of you has company coming and the house needs to be cleaned, laundry done, and groceries purchased. Set aside something you need done and offer to pitch in to help. Simply say you want to help and ask which of the jobs you can take over. This gesture will show your mate that you really care by sacrificing your time.

334. _Love Means Having to Say You Are Sorry_

If you make a mistake by doing or saying something that is hurtful or damaging to the relationship, say that you are sorry. Many people struggle with these words, even when they know that what they did was wrong. It actually takes a strong person to apologize. Do not wait until you think you have the courage but say it immediately, and with sincerity. Too often when couples argue, there is a long period of silence, which actually makes the anger and tension worse. You need to let your mate know immediately that you made a mistake and ask for forgiveness.

335. _Be Yourself_

Do not be phony in your relationship, trying to be someone or something different as a way to please your mate. For a relationship to work, both people need to be themselves and react to things naturally. Just imagine if you are really kind of on the silly side, enjoying life to the fullest. Then you meet a wonderful person who is much more conservative than you are. Because you are attracted to them, you try to squelch your normal vibrant personality. You are miserable and eventually, the person is going to be exposed to the "real" you. You have to base any relationship on honesty or it will eventually fall apart.

336. *Maintain Your Health*

You might think – what does good health have to do with a good relationship? In reality, it has a lot to do with it. Having a good relationship means having the energy to enjoy getting out and doing things together. To do that, it is important to eat right. When people are tired, they become short-tempered and frustrated. For this reason, it is important to get the right amount of sleep. Good exercise keeps your body in shape for being adventurous together. Taking care of your body and mind will flow over into your relationship and make you a calmer, stronger, and better-balanced person.

337. *Compliment – A Lot*

Be generous with compliments. It is very common for people to notice something nice about another person and think about it internally, but never voice it. When in a relationship, compliments are like glue. They hold the couple's attention and respect. Make sure your compliments are genuine and based on something you see or hear your mate do. If you have a clogged garbage disposal and your boyfriend or husband is able to unclog it, compliment them on being handy. If your girlfriend or wife takes her mother to the doctor, compliment her on her generosity. The fact is that criticism is destructive and can very quickly tear a relationship apart. Just like the cliché, "If you do not have something nice to say, then do not say anything at all." This is very true – take notice of the good things your mate does and make it known to them that you see and appreciate those things.

338. *Realistic Expectations*

No matter how wonderful and flawless your mate seems, no one is perfect. Be careful about putting someone on a pedestal, especially in the early stages of your relationship. Make sure that the expectations you have for your mate and yourself are realistic. There are going to be differences in opinion, and probably some disagreements. Also, do not assume that your mate knows how you feel or what you think about something. When discussing something important to you, ensure that you both understand the same thing. The reality is that neither one of you is going to know exactly what the other one needs. As long as you do not expect them to read your mind and accept that this is a part of getting to know one another and communicating, you will be fine.

339. _Leave the Baggage Behind_

Every person on the face of the Earth has some kind of history, or "baggage", although at varying levels. Do not walk into a relationship with your arms loaded with that baggage. The past is the past. Even though there are things from the past that are hurtful, and even damaging, learn from those things and come out a better and stronger person. This allows you to step into a new relationship with better knowledge of what _not_ to do. Leave the baggage from the past alone, focus on today, and look forward to tomorrow.

340. _Do Not Repeat, Do Not Repeat, Do Not Repeat_

Learn from your mistakes. When something goes wrong and the two of you work through it, do not repeat the same mistake. Rather than dive right back into whatever it was you did or said, think before you act. At first, this will take some discipline but as you see positive results in the relationship, be encouraged that it is working.

341. _Go on a Date_

Especially for married couples, but even for some "dating" couples, start dating. Often people become very comfortable in their relationship and sitting around on the weekends, watching movies is about as exciting as it gets. Ask your mate out. For example, actually call them and ask, "If you do not have any plans for Saturday night, would you like to go to a concert with me?" It is crucial to relationships that they keep the fire alive by enjoying the act of dating. There are many people in long-term, successful marriages that will tell you they go out on dates every week, which has been a huge bonus for their relationship.

342. _Memory Box_

Start a memory box to store old movie tickets, brochures from cities visited, concert ticket stubs, old ski lift passes, cards attached to flowers received, old love notes or letters, birthday cards or anniversary cards from your mate, anything that the two of you did together. Every once in awhile, pull the box out and look at the items with your mate. Reminisce about each memento, and keep all the special times in your life close to your heart!

343. _Keep the Kids Out of It_

Whether married or dating, if there are kids involved, it is crucial that they are not used as pawns in any situation. For example, if your mate wants to get intimate and you are not in the mood, do not say, "I need to help the kids with their homework," or if something that needed to be done was not taken care of because you forgot, do not blame it on the kids by saying, "I was taking care of the kids and did not have time." In the first scenario, be honest with your mate and tell them that you are very tired and while intimacy is important, you would prefer to make sure the kids are in bed on time so the two of you can have some quality time together. This opens an honest line of communication and does not place ill feelings on the kids, especially since it is not their problem to begin with.

344. _Listen to How You Talk_

When working on your relationship, more than likely you and your mate have settled into a pattern of speaking to each other. It might be with short, blunt answers, heavy sighs as though bothered, or with negative remarks. Pay attention to not only your words spoken, but also the tone in which they are spoken. Be positive, cheery, and respond in a way that will confirm to your mate that you are listening and truly interested – that you have time to listen and communicate. In addition, add terms of endearment into your conversation. Instead of "Good morning," try, "Hi honey, good morning!"

345. *Making Love*

Intimacy is a huge part of a successful relationship. Choose a book from the bookstore and try to bring a little excitement into your relationship. Do not be afraid to experiment and learn new and exciting ways to please each other. Keeping intimacy alive is healthy and not a bad thing whatsoever!

346. *Turn the Computer Off*

Often the computer becomes a replacement for a lack of something in the relationship. It might be just surfing, playing games, or getting involved with websites that promote pornography. If you notice that your mate is spending more and more time on the computer, take this as a sign that even if not doing anything wrong, they are choosing to spend the time with the computer instead of you. In other words, use this as a sign that something is missing in your relationship. Start by talking and searching to confirm what it is bothering your mate and then work on making it better!

347. *Follow Tradition*

Keep some tradition in your marriage, which relates to the vows you took and the fact that marriage is sacred. Treat each anniversary as a celebration of your love and the time spent together. Follow the traditional anniversary gifts and see how creative you can be. The first year anniversary gift is paper. One husband bought his wife a beautiful Chinese drawing on rice paper, signed by the artist, and had it framed for her. Make this fun, exciting, and keep traditions alive.

348. *Control Your Anger*

Every relationship has difficulties, and sometimes, there can be some intense arguments. For the sake of your relationship and the love you have for your mate, keep your anger in check. First, when people are angry, hurtful words fly, usually not even meant. However, after spoken, it is too late to take them back – the damage is done. Another problem with anger is that the word "divorce" can easily be thrown around. You may not mean it, but you know it hurts, thus making you the winner of the argument. NEVER talk about divorce in your relationship, even if just teasing. If you need to go to another room to cool off, and then do that, but whatever you do, do not allow your anger to take control of your relationship.

349. *Financial Woes*

One of the main reasons other than fidelity that marriages fall apart is due to finances. When couples are struggling with money problems, tempers flare, frustration builds, drinking may start, and it is an all-around unhealthy situation. The minute there are any signs of financial difficulties, the two of you need to immediately sit down and figure out a plan on how to deal with the problem. If needed, go to see a financial consultant or a credit counseling service to help you get back on track. Do not allow your finances to get out of line or your relationship will certainly suffer.

350. *I Forgive You*

If something has happened in your relationship causing the trust to waiver, you will have many things to work through. When your mate has done something that requires you to forgive, you have to forgive, REALLY forgive. Once you have worked through the issue either together or with professional counseling, and you tell them that you forgive them, you can never hold that over them again. As an example, if your mate has had an affair and the two of you choose to work it out rather than throw the relationship away, once the problems are resolved and the forgiveness is said, it is done! This means that you cannot stalk your mate to ensure they are where they said they would be, call or page them throughout the day, constantly ask for reaffirmation of your relationship, it means that you forgive and put the past behind you and then move on in a new, strong, and healthy relationship. It will not be easy, but you can do it with the right help, attitude, and commitment.

351. *Fighting No-No*

While having disagreements is normal and sometimes when controlled, healthy for relationships, the place and degree of discussion are important. Keep your disagreements private. Being at a party or anywhere around family or friends and breaking into an argument is a great way to break down a relationship. Not only does it cause embarrassment for your mate, but it also puts a negative light on both of you from the people witnessing the fight. If you are in public and think you need to argue, at least find a quiet corner or separate room where you can discuss whatever it is bothering you.

352. *Strong Family Ties*

When in a relationship, not only are you involved with the love of your life, but also the family of your mate. It is important to build a strong, healthy relationship with the families as well. Even if you do not see them often, having a good connection with your mate's family will make life for everyone much better all the way around.

353. *Mentoring*

If you know of another couple from work or your church that has been married for many years and continued to have a strong relationship, ask them if they would mentor you. Being around positive influences and watching someone who leads by example is a great way to learn how to have a good relationship for yourself.

354. *12-Month Calendar*

As a special gift, have a 12-month calendar created with pictures of special times spent between the two of you. Arrange the pictures to coordinate with the months and then as a Christmas or birthday gift, or just as a special surprise, present it to your loved one.

355. *Something Handmade*

You do not have to be a world-renowned artist to make something homemade and special for the love of your life. Even making a special, personalized greeting card would be appreciated and show your mate that you care enough to take the time needed to make something by hand.

356. _Favorite Meal_

If your mate has a meal, that is by far the favorite above everything else, go all out and prepare everything to order. Before they arrive home, put on something nice and a little sexy, light some candles, and have a wonderful surprise waiting.

357. _Trip to the Pound_

If you and your mate love animals, take a trip to the local animal shelter and pick out a dog or cat that needs a good home. Adopting an animal that needs a home can be a wonderful way to have something that you both can care for and love together. This will open up for long walks, taking your new dog on a walk, or hours of playing with a sweet and funny cat.

358. _Day at the Movies_

Have a movie marathon some rainy or cold Saturday. Put all your errands and chores on hold and head to your nearest theater. Hit three or four movies and mix it up. Buy the theater popcorn and drinks but sneak your own candy in. This is a great way to spend some fun time together, holding hands or cuddling, while sharing some laughs and maybe tears watching a variety of flicks.

359. _A Walk in the Park_

Spending quality time together where you can talk and just enjoy each other's company is critical to a good relationship. Plan a nice walk in the park to include a comfortable blanket to sit on the grass with while having a good old-fashioned picnic. Take this time talk, watch other people with their kids, and then just walk around, hand-in-hand.

360. _Name a Star_

As a special gift, ask your mate to join you outside at night when the sky is black and the stars shining brightly. Point up to the universe and state, "See that star over there? That is your star. I bought it for you." Then present them with the certificate showing that they do in fact have a star named after them. This wonderful gift will last a lifetime!

361. _Coupon Book_

Create a coupon book filled with any number you like of 20-minute massages. One day when least expected, when your mate comes dragging in the door tired after a long, hard day at work, present this along with a gentle kiss. Although you are the one offering the massages, if you remain faithful to your coupons and never grumble, your love life will more than likely be enhanced and before long, your mate will be the one giving you massages.

362. _Dinner by the Fire_

Order in some of your favorite food, open a bottle of fine wine, light some candles, and lay out a cozy blanket in front of a roaring fire. Enjoy feeding each other food, sneaking little kisses in between. This wonderful romantic moment will help build your relationship even stronger. This kind of gesture shows your mate that you really want something special from your relationship and that spending quality time together is a priority.

363. _Scavenger Hunt_

If things have been a little stressed in your relationship, do something extra special. Start by creating a trail of rose petals from the door to the kitchen where your mate will find a note to go to the bedroom. In the bedroom, have another note next to an overnight bag telling them to meet you at a specific hotel restaurant where you know the ambience is cozy and romantic. The note should direct them to ask for you at the restaurant where you will be waiting to enjoy a fine dinner together. After dinner and cocktails, gently lead your mate by the hand to a beautiful room that you have reserved for the night. There on the bed is a robe and a red rose. This will do more for your relationship than you can imagine.

364. *Photo Album*

As a wonderful keepsake, create a photo album for your mate. Include the parents or siblings to come up with some special childhood and teenage pictures. Include family, friends, special occasions, and times of the two of you together. Whenever the two of you feel as though you are drifting apart or taking one another for granted, pull out the photo album as a reminder of the incredible person in your life.

365. *The Art of Gift Giving*

Everyone loves to be given a gift, especially as a surprise or "just because." Just remember while giving gifts is a beautiful thing to do for the person you love, there are five key essentials for making your mate know that you are giving just because you love them. First, put some thought into the gift. Do not just pick up something at the last minute so you are not empty handed. Second, make the effort. Even if you have a busy schedule, be sure to schedule time to shop. Third, give with the right attitude. You give because you appreciate and love, not because you want something back. Fourth, plan what you are going to give. Find something that is important for your mate and not necessarily to you. Finally, add the element of surprise into the gift giving. Using this equation is sure to impress your mate and leave a lasting impression.

366. *Family History*

Perform some extensive research on your mate's family history, which will involve some help from the family, and create a website especially for your mate's family where they can share information, pictures, family recipes, and more! This will take some time and planning but very little money.

Myfamily.com is a great site that is extremely reasonable. This will not only touch your mate's heart, but the hearts of the entire family.

367. <u>*A Day at the Spa*</u>

For couples where the mother or father stays home and takes care of the children all day long, show your appreciation for the hard work that takes. Hire a babysitter for about four hours and give your mate a gift certificate to a local spa where they can enjoy a relaxing massage, mineral springs, sauna, mud wrap, or whatever special treatments are available.

368. <u>*Charity*</u>

Find a charity that you would both like to contribute to and give something special in both names. For example, if there is a synergy house near where you live for unwed mothers, go in together and purchase a crib or baby clothes. Another option would be if a local park needs donations, find out what kind of trees they need and purchase a tree together. Make this something special where you go shop together and then present together. These types of kind acts are great for bringing couples closer together and help both people love and appreciate each other even more for their kindness.

369. <u>*Thunderstorms*</u>

While some people find thunderstorms to be scary, they can also be viewed as being romantic. If you have having a thunderstorm in your area, without putting yourself in harm's way, sit out on your porch if the storm is still off in the distance, or cuddled on the couch near a large window and just watch the lightening together.

370. <u>*Take Pride in Yourself*</u>

Every relationship goes through down time. Just because the flame has become a mild flicker, that does not mean you have lost the love for each other, it just means you need to add a little fuel to the fire. When couples have been together for a long time, the makeup comes off, the nice clothes turn into oversized sweats and tee shirts, and instead of cuddling on the sofa or floor, one sits on the couch and the other in the recliner. Step back in time and start getting dressed up more on the weekends, invite your mate to sit with you on the couch, dance together in your living room to some music, or take a walk, hand in hand. It is important not to let yourself go, even when your relationship reaches a "comfortable" state. By taking pride in yourself means that you take pride in your relationship.

371. *No Jealousy Allowed*

To have a healthy relationship, caring and concern are fine but when those emotions change into jealousy, this could be the beginning of trouble. Trust is probably the number one element needed in order to have a strong relationship. Without trust, things will quickly deteriorate. If one of you masters something special, receives a promotion at work, or achieves some great feat, there could be a small spark of jealousy on the other person's side. You need to talk about this and ensure that any feelings of inadequacies are permanently put to rest. Every person needs assurance at some time or another and as long as you can communicate, things will be fine. However, if your mate becomes withdrawn or irritated, these could be signs that more is going on. Once jealousy enters a relationship, problems are soon to follow.

372. *Keep in Touch*

If you are in a relationship, where your mate serves in the armed forces and is overseas or in another state on duty, away in a foreign country for school, or separated from you for one reason or another, it is important that you keep in touch with each other often. There will be stress from the separation but by keeping in touch and informing each other of the things each person is dealing with, how they feel, etc., you will not have any break in your communication. The goal is that when you get back together, you can easily pick up where you left off. This is a very important time to provide each other with confirmation of your love and validation of your relationship. While this will require some extra effort on both parts, keep in mind that the separation is not forever.

373. *Host a Halloween Party*

Instead of just passing out candy for Halloween, organize a masquerade party together where everyone is required to come dressed up. Include in your party food, drinks, door prizes, and games. Have a few friends provide help you plan this and then go all out. Choose costumes the two of you can wear to enhance each other. A few suggestions would be to Adam and Eve (wearing skin-toned clothing – no nudity), Batman and Batgirl, Cleopatra and Marc Anthony, Romeo and Juliet, Robin Hood and Maid Marian, or Sonny and Cher. You will have a blast with the planning and searching out your costumes. This type of party is great for good laughs and fond memories of each other, which are important for a good relationship.

374. *Special Music*

Select numerous songs that your mate would enjoy and have them either recorded on a cassette or burned on a CD that can be enjoyed while driving to and from work. To add a little spice, record a few secret messages every few songs just reminding them how much you love and appreciate them.

375. *New Adventures*

Arrange for the two of you to try something new *together*. If you are both the athletic type, enter yourselves into some type of physical competition. If the two of you like the fine arts, audition for roles in a local community theater. Perhaps you like to travel. If so, arrange for a short trip to some place exotic that you have never been before.

376. *Adopt a Family*

When the Christmas holiday starts getting closer, locate a family together from your church or local charity services that needs to be adopted for Christmas. Together, shop for the gifts, and have the family over for the most scrumptious holiday dinner. You will both appreciate what you have even more as well as your own special relationship.

377. *Getting Married*

If your relationship has moved to a set wedding date and the countdown has started, do something unique and fun. Visit a candy store and have 30-miniature candy hearts made, each with a special message of love. Each day, present your mate with the appropriate candy heart. As you get down to the final days before the wedding, they might read something like, "Only two more days", "Tomorrow: The Big Day", "I love you, your wife (or husband)."

378. *Motivate Each Other*

Find a mutual incentive that will motivate both of you to being the best you can be. Find something that you can both be excited about and then attach some type of reward to the motivation. If one of you has had a dream of writing a screenplay, make that your goal and take that on together. The motivation is that when finished, the two of you will take a beautiful, romantic weekend vacation to some exotic place. The goal could be anything that is important to one person or both and that can be worked toward completion together. Another example would be if your mate has always dreamed of buying an old model car and restoring it do it together and then take a special trip to the Indy 500 as your reward. Yet another example might be to restore a home. Make this a joint project and then as a reward, add a Jacuzzi into your plans. Use your imagination and enjoy the venture together.

379. *Embrace Change*

There is no relationship on the face of the planet that goes for years and years without change. People change as they mature and view life differently, therefore reacting differently. Rather than get upset with each other over change, embrace change. You may not always like the changes that happen, but do not throw away a perfectly good relationship just because the trail starts to wind. Be patient and encourage new directions while being honest about concerns that might arise.

380. _Reap What You Sow_

This is an old saying that goes back a very long way but it still holds true today. If you sow love, forgiveness, faithfulness, encouragement, honesty, and acceptance, then that is what you will reap. It is definitely true that what you put into a relationship is what you get back.

381. _Board Games_

Pick a night, perhaps on a cold winter night, and just enjoy playing board games. This can be with just the two of you, or with several close friends. Bring out the snacks, beverages, and just have some fun. Laughter and fun are important factors in any relationship, for any age. Laugh and enjoy having a good time with good honest fun! You will truly be amazed at what this can do for your relationship.

382. _No Interference_

Do not allow other people to interfere with your relationship. If family members try to get in the middle of fights or debates, that is definite trouble. You might have friends with well-meant intentions trying to help you and your mate solve problems. Although getting another person's perspective is not a bad thing, make sure it is when you ask for it. It is very important to keep integrity in your relationship and not allow people to interfere.

383. _Adore your Mate_

Beyond telling your mate that you love them, that they are special, and having passion in your relationship, you shou d adore your mate and what they bring into the relationship. What that means is to appreciate and love them for the person they are, faults and all. This is true devotion to your mate and demonstration that you do not take them for granted.

384. *Follow Your Instincts*

When things are going in a wrong direction, often people will simply keep going in the same direction while hoping that things work themselves out. The result is usually negative. Instead, listen to your gut feelings, your inner instincts. If you believe that something is bothering your mate or not right in your relationship, keep it between you and your mate and work things out as a couple.

385. *Be Creative*

The words, "I love you," are always welcomed but why not add some creativity to the way you tell your mate you love them. Rent a billboard in a location where you know your mate drives every day that clearly says, "I love you," request that your mate's radio station play a special song and message on his or her way to work, or if celebrating a special anniversary, have a skywriter fly by a ball stadium, park, or somewhere special where you are spending quality time together outdoors.

386. *Make Eye Contact*

You may not think this is important, but think back to the first time you saw your now mate. More than likely, the first interaction was through eye contact. If you are having dinner during the holidays with a large group of family and friends, glance over to your mate and give them a seductive wink, or if your mate is giving a speech and you are there to offer support, attentively look at them, making directly eye contact and offer a warm reassuring smile. Eyes can say a lot!

387. *Learn More about Your Mate*

Either find a good questionnaire or create one that does not dig up the past, but focuses on discovering other qualities about each other. One happily married couple did this and the wife, who had been standing by her husband for more than 10 years, discovered that he used to be a competitive ice skater. She had no idea. Guess what they did on Saturday?

388. *Change Routines*

Understand that every once in a wh le, it is important to throw an exciting curve into your relationship. If you are in a routine for example of offering your mate a quick peck on the lips before you part ways for the day, try adding a soft, gentle kiss on the neck. You can be assured that throughout the day, that change in routine, is what will be on your mate's mind.

389. *Dance*

Finding a nice place where the two of you can enjoy a slow dance is a great way to spend time together, holding each other without saying a word. Keep in mind that to accomplish this, you can stay home and simply move some furniture out of the way, light some candles, and put on your favorite soft music and enjoy some quiet, romantic time together.

390. *Sunrise/Sunset*

Too often people miss the beautiful miracle of a sunrise or sunset. Schedule time to get up early one morning with a thermos of hot coffee or cappuccino and find a quiet place where the two of you can go just to watch the sun rise or set. Appreciate what nature has to offer and share it with each other.

391. *Explorations*

Find something they you are both interested in exploring and do it together. For example, if you live in a place where there are caves, make a day of driving around and exploring caves. Be sure to take the right equipment and safety precautions but this puts you both in a position of trusting each other and discovering something new and exciting together.

392. _To Tell or Not to Tell_

Experts will disagree on how much of a person's past should be shared in a relationship and while some things probably should be shared, most people lean more to not sharing every aspect of the past. First, it is the past. Think back to how much people grow through the teen years to mid-twenties. Offering unnecessary information from the past is a great way to create distrust, insecurity, and more questions than answers. Be wise when sharing.

393. _Respect Privacy_

When two people come together in a relationship, each person has their own set of history. There are yearbooks, maybe love letters from a first love, other objects that may not seem important to one person but to the owner, they have a special meaning. It is important to respect the privacy of your mate's "stuff." Do not dig through boxes of things owned by your mate out of curiosity. Instead, allow them to bring those things out if they feel it is necessary. By helping yourself, you are disrespecting something sacred to your mate, which is not healthy for any relationship.

394. _No Place for Abuse_

Regardless of how much you love your mate and believe in who they are, there is NEVER an appropriate time for abuse, whether physical, emotional, or verbal. If your mate shows aggression or any form of abuse toward you, seek counseling for both of you immediately to try to work through things. If your mate refuses to go, even if it is hard, leave. First is your safety. Second, it is possible for people to learn ways in which to manage their aggressions. If this is the case, the life of the relationship has a much better chance of surviving!

395. _Open Your Eyes_

Do not drive yourself crazy with this, but take notice of how your relationship is going. Open your eyes and take stock of what is and is not working in your relationship. Are there definite things missing or definite problem areas that need to be worked on?   Think about it. If you invest in the stock market, you pay attention to what is going on so you can make changes if needed. Your relationship is far more than the stock market but requires some of the same strategies.

396. *The Grass is NOT Greener!*

Too many times, people get tired of working on the relationship they are currently in and feel that by moving on to another person, they will find greener pastures. This is just not the case. What happens is when you move to another person, things are fresh, new, and exciting just as they were in the beginning of your current relationship. Within time, that relationship will also start experiencing differences and bumps in the road. Unless you are being abused or your mate is doing something illegal or completely irresponsible, perhaps the efforts you would put into starting a new relationship would be better spent fixing the one you have.

397. *Start a Journal*

Keep your personal feelings and discoveries about your mate in a journal. This will help to remember what special things he or she likes or dislikes, track the wonderful times spent together, and help you to feel better when you hit an obstacle in your relationship. When things get a little tough, refer to your journal and read through all the terrific emotions and time together and you will find plenty of reasons to make things right again.

398. *Be Flexible*

Remember that relationships are give and take situations, not competition between two people who love each other. There will be times when your mate is right and times when you are right. When you feel the conversation getting a little on the edgy side with each of you trying to hold ground, do not forget that there can be many ways to accomplish the same task. The result is that each of you might learn something new from the other person. Put your heads together and do what makes the most sense instead of battling for ownership of the solution.

399. *Cut out the Excuses*

A major turn-off in many situations, not only relationships, is people who have an excuse for everything. Forget that. Do not make excuses in fear of your mate not liking, loving, or respecting you. Be yourself and if you messed up with something, just admit to it. Say you had promised to make dinner, got home exhausted, and just did not feel like making it, do not tell your mate, "I had to work overtime." Be honest and say, "You know, I got home after a busy day and I was too tired. What sounds better, Chinese or Pizza?" This has taken you out of the situation of lying and reconfirmed your honest nature to your mate.

400. *Spirituality*

Statistics show that couples that spend time in church together usually have strong relationships. Bringing spirituality into your relationship is important. Allow the love of God to be your ultimate guide and spend time having devotions together at night. If you are just starting out dating, religious preference may not seem like a big deal at first, but soon into the relationship, it can be a big trouble spot. Make time for God in your life and consider dating someone who shares the same faith!

401. *Learn to be Successful*

Many couples are starting to go to counseling or relationship/marriage classes much earlier in their relationship rather than waiting until after the marriage is in trouble. This is a great option for learning how to have a healthy, lasting relationship and develop open communication.

402. *Work and Home Do Not Mingle*

How many times have you heard this? It is true. While sharing experiences about your day with your mate is perfectly normal, living your work at home is not. If you have to bring work home, set a specific amount of time it will take you to complete, let your mate know, and then when quitting time comes, quit! It is important to separate the two parts of your life and keep you work at the job, and when at home, pay attention to your mate and/or family.

403. *Encourage Friendships*

Men, unlike women, have a more difficult time in developing close friendships with other men. This is a natural part of life and while they may have some buddies from high school or college that they see on occasion, rarely do they set specific time aside just for friends. Men and women both need an outlet outside of the relationship where they can just "let their guard down" and have some fun with the same gender. As your mate makes new friendships, encourage that growth and show 100% support!

404. *Confidentiality*

Women are usually blessed with the gift of gab, making it easy, sometimes too easy, to talk to other people. Keep information shared to you by your mate in 100% confidence. Unless they have told you of a crime they have committed, they are confiding in you and placing full trust in your relationship. All it takes is one time of spilling private information for the entire relationship to suffer.

As you can see, relationships take work. However, with the right attitude, a lot of hard work, and some unique ideas on how to make is successful, couples can have a strong, lifelong relationship!